Better Homes and Gardens®

Decorative Painting

STEP-BY-STEP

Meredith® Books
Des Moines, Iowa

TABLE OF CONTENTS

Planning
FOR DECORATIVE PAINTING   6

Selecting
COLORS AND TECHNIQUES   22

Decorative
PAINTING TECHNIQUES   34

Tools
AND MATERIALS
130

Painting
BASICS
142

INTRODUCTION

Few home-improvement projects achieve quicker results and make greater impact for the money you invest than decorative paint treatments. Decorative painting, when done correctly and consistently, boosts the character and appearance of your home. Faux (false) finishes enable you to inexpensively mimic the look of luxury building materials, such as marble, granite, and fine hardwoods. Additionally, taking on decorative paint projects yourself enables you to personalize walls, floors, ceilings, furniture, and other surfaces with your signature style and colors. Plus, doing the work yourself can save a considerable amount of money compared with hiring a professional faux-finish painter.

Beautiful decorative painting effects were once the realm of experienced professional painters.

Fortunately, today's do-it-yourselfers can find dozens of high-quality, reasonably priced tools and materials at most paint stores and home centers. It has never before been easier to achieve professional-looking results. All you need are the right tools and materials, an understanding of the basic techniques, and a bit of practice.

Better Homes and Gardens® Decorative Painting Step-by-Step shows you everything you need to achieve beautifully painted walls. You'll learn about paint treatments, tools, and how-to techniques you need to achieve professional-looking results.

How to Use This Book

This book's five parts are arranged to help you dream about, organize, plan, and execute your decorative painting projects. "Planning for Decorative Painting" (page 6) introduces you to the ever-expanding world of decorative paint finishes by taking you on a tour of fantastic finished rooms and techniques. "Selecting Colors and Techniques" (page 22) helps you select colors, tools, paints, and glazes for your projects like a professional designer. You also learn how to select treatments for specific rooms and surfaces. "Decorative Painting Techniques" (page 34), the third and most extensive part of the book, takes you step-by-step through decorative painting techniques. Special motion-capture photos show the movements and hand positions that give great results. Then, "Tools and Materials" (page 130) and "Painting Basics" (page 142) get you up to speed on essential supplies you need to have on hand, and the core skills for applying paint to walls and trim.

Jump to the section that best suits your needs and let the decorative painting begin!

Tip Boxes

In addition to the basic instructions you'll find throughout this book, "You'll Need" boxes at the start of each decorative painting technique outline the time, skills, tools, and materials required. Pay attention to the "Caution" boxes, which alert you to situations that could lead to danger or disappointing results. Other information boxes provide helpful hints, project planning insights, and additional decorating ideas.

TURN YOUR IMAGINATION LOOSE
Apply decorative painting techniques to walls, cabinetry, furniture, or any other surface to create a unique look.

SAFETY PRECAUTIONS

Decorative painting is a relatively safe home-improvement activity. However, you can get into a few potentially dangerous situations.

Protect yourself with appropriate clothing and safety gear while painting. Wear loose, old clothing or purchase paint overalls or coveralls. Wear a respirator and cloth gloves while sanding or stripping any surface before painting. Cover your eyes with protective goggles or safety glasses when sanding or painting overhead. Because some decorative techniques require prolonged direct contact with paint and solvents, wear disposable or washable rubber gloves. Always wear comfortable rubber-soled shoes when painting.

Before you sand or strip old paint—particularly if you find pre-1978, light-color paint below more recent top coats—test for lead. Lead test kits are easy to use, inexpensive, and available at home centers and paint stores. If you find that your home contains lead paint, do not remove it. Contact the Environmental Protection Agency (EPA) at 1-800-424-LEAD or www.epa.gov for advice.

Because all paints and solvents, even those labeled "nontoxic," release some amount of toxic vapors and particles into the air, always work in a well-ventilated space. Open doors and windows and run a fan to help remove vapors and particles. Wear a mask or respirator if you're particularly sensitive.

Take special care whenever working on any ladder. When in use a stepladder should be fully opened, with all legs making firm contact with the floor. If your ladder features a locking mechanism, always secure the latch before standing on the ladder.

For additional information on safety gear to have on hand, turn to page 134.

PAINT HIGHER SAFELY
When decoratively painting from a stepladder, you should be able to reach any area easily. Avoid painting from the top two steps of the ladder; get a taller ladder instead.

PLAN AND PRACTICE
With careful planning, a little practice, and high-quality materials, you can achieve professional decorative painting results on your walls, floors, ceilings, and furniture.

Planning
FOR DECORATIVE PAINTING

There are many reasons to include decorative painting treatments in your home. Decorative paint treatments are the easiest, most cost-effective way to add a personal, custom look to your rooms and furnishings.

Decorative painting lets you get the look of linen, brick, or wood without installing the actual materials. Even European nobility knew the power of decorative painting, hiring faux-finish painters to embellish ordinary surfaces with treatments that mimicked more expensive materials. If it worked for them, it can work for you.

By combining paint with plaster, sand, or other solid additives, decorative paint techniques add intriguing texture, as well as color and sheen, to a surface. Textured surfaces can disguise wall imperfections.

Decorative paint treatments applied strategically to a room or throughout an entire home can highlight specific surfaces or architectural features, such as fireplaces, windows, doors, and built-in cabinetry, creating focal points in otherwise unimpressive spaces. Decorative paint treatments also can help clearly differentiate areas, rooms, and functions in your home.

STRIPES AND TEXTURES

Marking off stripes with painter's tape and dragging a rubber comb through white glaze give this wall rich, contrasting color and intriguing texture. For more on combing, turn to pages 57–59.

MADE-UP MARBLE

Faux marbling transforms a brand-new fireplace surround into an architectural focal point that seems rich in history and craftsmanship. For more on marbling, turn to page 94.

STENCILING

Stenciled designs over a solid-color or textured background add interest to walls. For more on stenciling methods, turn to pages 100–106.

GALLERY OF TECHNIQUES

The wide range of decorative painting techniques practiced today includes treatments that resemble fabric, stone, or wood, and those that simply impart varying texture and color to a surface.

These six pages introduce you to some of the most popular decorative painting techniques. and instruct you where to turn in the book for how-to details for creating similar looks yourself.

FAUX STONE
With naturalistic details, like grout lines, rough texturing, and even small cracks, this painted floor resembles a rustic stone-inlaid floor. See page 90 for stone-painting techniques.

RAGGING OFF
Ragging off allows the base-coat color to shine subtly through a glaze top coat in a few areas, imparting a warm, worn effect. Here, a darker tangerine top-coat glaze has been ragged off, revealing a glimpse of a lighter yellow base coat. For more ragging techniques, turn to page 48.

STRIPES

The loose stripes on the walls of this sunny bedroom were applied by hand. The slight irregularity lends a look of casual elegance. Tips for stripes are on page 118.

STAMPING AND TAPING

Painter's tape and premade stamps are the only tools necessary to create a dining room with inviting color and crisp graphic interest. For more on stamping, turn to page 122.

COMBING

Combing vertically and horizontally through red glaze that's been applied atop a cream base coat creates an intriguing burlap effect. For more on various combing techniques, turn to page 57.

Gallery of Techniques *(continued)*

FAUX FABRIC
More practical and cost-effective than upholstering bathroom walls with yards of denim, this wall technique pairs a stiff wire roller with two shades of blue paint. Overlapping the sections boosts the fabric-mimicking effect, creating the appearance of seams. For more on denim techniques, turn to page 65.

DISTRESSING
Various distressing techniques give this new wood cabinet the look and feel of a family heirloom. For more on distressing, turn to page 74.

AGING AND ANTIQUING
Various aging techniques around the moldings, window frames, and archway in this home office provide a weathered contrast to the refined furniture. See page 70.

SPONGING
Light glaze sponged on the tops of walls painted deep gold gives the illusion of textured Old World walls. For more on sponging, turn to page 44.

VENETIAN PLASTER
The rich color, luster, and texture of Venetian plaster help this space feel like an elegant Italian villa rather than a modern-day suburban home. For more on Venetian plaster, turn to page 126.

Gallery of Techniques *(continued)*

COLOR WASHING
A basic color wash of yellow over a slightly deeper base coat makes this living room glow with warmth. For more on color washing, turn to page 36.

FAUX MARBLE
A bookshelf gets a fast facelift by applying faux marble panels and crisp, white trim to salmon-painted cabinetry. For more on faux marble, turn to page 94.

LINEN

The soft and subtle linen technique in this sitting room was created with layers of glaze and stiff brushes. For more on linen looks, turn to page 62.

COMPLEX COLOR WASHING

A more complex color wash in this entryway combines eight different colors—three shades of green, two shades of amber, two shades of ivory, and lavender—into one custom treatment. For more on color washing, turn to page 36.

ROOM BY ROOM:
FAMILY-FRIENDLY FINISHES

Family rooms, living rooms, and dens are a few of the more popular rooms where homeowners incorporate decorative painting techniques. These gathering spaces offer ideal venues for decorative paint techniques, making the rooms warm and welcoming for family and friends. And because these are public rooms, guests get to enjoy the fruits of your labors as well.

COMFY FAMILY ROOM
The walls in this family room serve as a soothing contrast to the chocolate-brown upholstery and also provide a richly textured background for displaying art. Double rolling enables you to apply and blend two paint colors at one time. For more on double-rolling techniques, turn to page 54.

QUIET CORNER
Sueded walls make this corner a comfortable spot for homework or household bill-paying. You can achieve the look of soft, supple suede on your walls by using specially formulated suede paint (available at paint stores and home centers) or by following our special technique described on page 82.

ROOM BY ROOM: HARDWORKING TREATMENTS

Many paint treatments are as durable as they are decorative—a combination that's especially important in rooms that require attractive yet easy-to-clean surfaces. Even delicate paint treatments can gain additional durability by applying a coat or two of clear matte polyurethane. If you have questions about the appropriateness or durability of a treatment or product, consult with a paint store professional.

COUNTRY KITCHEN
Distressing techniques applied to bold red and yellow cabinets make this suburban kitchen feel as cozy as a French country cottage. For a variety of distressing techniques and ideas, turn to page 74.

DRAMATIC DINING
A dining room that lacks architectural interest becomes a regal and dramatic space, thanks to a color wash of three different shades of purple, and a curlicue stencil made with white pearlized paint.

ELEGANT ENTRY
Because everybody sees it, an entry foyer is a great place to show off your finest decorative painting techniques. These green and cream stripes combine three techniques: Taping creates the striped effect; ragging off, the mottled green stripes; and stenciling, the thistle motif.

ROOM BY ROOM: RELAXING AND REVIVING

Personal spaces, such as bedrooms and bathrooms, give you a chance to experiment with bolder treatments, unusual color combinations, and specialty products. Lavish these private rooms with as much attention as you give your high-traffic areas. And because these spaces are truly yours, you can make your color and treatment choices as personal as you desire.

> ### BLUE SKY
> Blue color-washed walls provide a perfect background for sponge-painted clouds and a stenciled border of trains and planes. For more stenciling ideas, turn to page 100.

> ### BOXY DESIGN
> Multicolor squares bring a dynamic contemporary look to this bedroom. Random arrangement of colors adds interest. For more on gridded designs, turn to page 120.

STENCILS BY THE SINK
Two stamps in two shades of pink paint provide a whimsical cottage look for a basic bathroom. For more about stamping, turn to page 122.

SWEET STRIPES
The simple and sweet wall treatment in this girl's room combines taped stripes and floral stencils for an effect that mimics painted paneling.

Expand your decorative painting horizons by including floors and ceilings along with traditional walls in your painting plans. But you don't have to stop there: Any surface that you can paint is a possible canvas for decorative treatments. Consider trimwork, doors, moldings, and just about any piece of furniture an opportunity to apply your decorative painting skills.

FABULOUS FLOOR
Whitewashing and painting a grid of large diamonds in an entryway can be an inexpensive way to save wood floors that require extensive refinishing.

VANITY FAIR
Stenciled relief, combining traditional stencils and layers of plaster, creates raised details and texture on a bathroom vanity. For more on stenciled relief, turn to page 103.

∧

WOOD-GRAINED METAL
A basic metal filing cabinet takes on the look of richly grained oak by running a rubber graining tool through a series of brown glazes. Turn to page 98 for more on faux wood graining.

∧

PALM CANOPY
Large-scale palm fronds stenciled in a ceiling inset above a dining table give this dining room an eye-elevating finishing touch.

<

COTTAGE DOORWAY
A new five-panel door gains instant cottage charm with a quick coat of whitewash. A delicate vine stenciled border applied around the frame adds a vintage touch. See page 72 for more on whitewashing; turn to page 100 for stenciling.

Selecting
COLORS AND TECHNIQUES

Achieving great final results with your decorative painting projects requires more than just learning how to hold a sea sponge, wring out a chamois cloth, or operate a double roller. Although decorative painting techniques and skills are important to learn and develop, knowing a little about color, paints, glazes, and basic design principles can make all your hard work pay off in a beautiful finished room in which all the surfaces, furniture, architectural details, and lighting work together in harmony.

This section illustrates the decorating and design basics necessary to confidently achieve a complete look. Learn how to identify rooms, walls, and furniture pieces that are best-suited for decorative painting. Select appropriate decorative paint techniques and treatments for specific surfaces. Gather and purchase high-quality tools and materials based on your home improvement budget. Combine colors, sheens, textures, and techniques like a professional designer. Prepare any surface—walls, floors, ceilings, trim, furniture, and more—to receive paint.

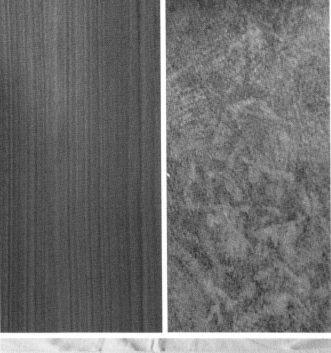

> **CONSISTENT STYLE**
By combining consistent decorative painting techniques with carefully selected colors and paint products, you'll be amazed at the enduring style you can introduce into your home.

ENDLESS COLOR
The range of colors available at home centers and paint stores may overwhelm you. Remembering some basic definitions and decorating guidelines helps you sift through the color chaos and find the perfect hues for your project. <

> **PAINT PARTS**
Most paint is made of four parts: liquid, pigments, additives, and binders. Liquid (water in latex paints; mineral spirits in oil) makes paint easy to apply. Pigments give paint color. Additives give the paint additional capabilities, such as scrubability or sun-resistance. Binders bond pigment and additives to the surface.

PICKING YOUR PAINT PROJECTS

Decorative painting may be a cost-effective decorating solution, but the process still requires some investment for high-quality tools and supplies, as well as considerable time and effort. Most likely, you're going to live with your decorative painting choices for several years. For these reasons, take special care when selecting the rooms, surfaces, and furniture that you plan to paint.

Stroll through the rooms in your home and consider all the walls, floors, ceilings, trimwork, and furniture. Could any of these surfaces benefit from applying a decorative paint treatment? Understanding the effect of certain choices will help you select the best options. Generally, decorative paint treatments can have a dramatic impact on these areas:

- *Perceived ceiling height.* A ceiling featuring an elaborate paint treatment or dark color draws the eye upward, making the ceiling seem lower and closer. This effect can be helpful if you have tall ceilings or you want to give a room greater warmth and intimacy.
- *Perceived room size.* Decorative paint treatments tend to make rooms feel somewhat smaller. This is helpful if you have a large room or desire a space to feel cozier and more special.
- *The focus of the room.* Because decorative paint treatments attract the eye, applying a treatment to a single wall or architectural feature generally makes that place the focal point of the room. Be sure you highlight the walls and features that you want to command special attention.
- *The consistency of your entire home.* The right decorative paint treatment can unify a mismatched dining set, or link your kitchen and living room into one multifunctional space. Contrasting treatments in different spaces have the effect of separating them even more than architectural barriers that are already in your floor plan.

> **COMBINED TECHNIQUES**
> To achieve a look that mixes multiple decorative painting techniques in one room you need to apply appropriate treatments to the specific surfaces, establish a consistent color scheme, and allow some surfaces (the floors and the windows in this living room) to be simple and unadorned.

After selecting a surface to paint, shift your focus to choosing the best decorative treatment for that surface. While you need to weigh your options for your situation, a few tried-and-true design guidelines can help you make the best decisions possible.

When using treatments that mimic another material, choose treatments that make logical sense. While you certainly could paint your cabinet doors to resemble granite bricks, you'd never find granite cabinets in the real world!

Consider how the surface you're planning to paint will be used. Furniture, trim, and cabinetry require more durable products and treatments. Treatments with raised texture or porous finishes usually are less durable and attract more dust and dirt than flat finishes. Treatments involving delicate details or easily damaged materials should be confined to low-traffic spaces. While you always can consider adding a few coats of clear polyurethane on top of a finished treatment for protection, polyurethane can subtly alter the color or perceived detail, diminishing the effect of some treatments.

Consider how the room you're going to paint connects to other spaces. If the room links visually to another space via archways, a flowing floor plan, or large windows, you need to take the decor of both spaces into account when making color and treatment choices.

Most important, avoid faux overload. There can be too much of a good thing! Every surface in a room does not require a decorative paint treatment. In fact, most paint treatments gain greater prominence and have more impact when paired with solid-color fabrics, floor coverings, and paints.

COORDINATED COLORS
Coordinating an elaborate paint treatment with a solid wall color is a good way to make the treatment seem even more special and to avoid too many textures. Here, a dragging technique is applied to the deep green dining room walls, while sunny yellow provides a bright but neutral backdrop.

You can find the supplies, tools, and products necessary to complete all the decorative paint treatments featured in this book at a paint store or home center.

Savvy Shopping

When purchasing supplies for a decorative paint project, take your time and plan ahead. Whenever possible, shop during less-busy hours and try to avoid the mass of weekend do-it-yourselfers that flood home centers. You need adequate time to compare colors, tools, and supplies to ensure that you get everything you need for a project and that you make the best choices possible.

When you shop, take along a folder or gallon-size plastic bag with samples of any paint, fabric, stain, or other materials you need to consider as you select colors and supplies. This packet should also include measurements of all the areas you plan to paint (see "Paint Quantities," *at right,* for information on estimating paint quantities quickly and accurately). Other helpful items to take along in your planning packet are shopping checklists, book or magazine images of treatment examples, and instructions for the techniques you think may work for your surfaces.

Most decorative painting decisions are driven by color or a specific technique. Go with whichever aspect of the project seems most important to you.

If you know the technique you're planning to try, find out how many paint colors you need to do the treatment. Pay attention to how much contrast is required between colors. Find out what types and quantities of glazes or other additives you need. Packaging labels on glaze products or discussions with store employees will help you determine the ideal paint products and tools to combine with various glazes.

If color is driving your decorative painting project, start in the paint section and look over the colors available. Many decorative painting techniques require multiple colors or shades to achieve a full effect. Fortunately, this means you don't have to find the one perfect color for your project.

Many paint manufacturers now sell paint and glazes along with other decorative additives. While it can be easier to work within one manufacturer's line of paints and glazes for a project, you can use paints, glazes, and additive products from various manufacturers in the same project. Let your decorating needs—not the marketing efforts of paint manufacturers—drive your choices. See page 28 for more tips on selecting colors.

Decorative paint treatments require good paints. They cost more, but are easier to apply, are more durable, have truer color, and provide better coverage. Price often is the most reliable indicator of quality, so be prepared to purchase more expensive paint.

Most decorative paint techniques require at least a few specialty tools or applicators. You can find decorative painting tools at most home centers and paint stores. Often, decorative paints, glazes, and tools are displayed together and feature common branding or instructions. Although working from the preselected options can save time and guarantee more predictable results, let your color and texture needs determine your purchase choices.

With some ingenuity, you can often modify inexpensive tools to perform the duties of costlier decorative painting tools. For example, stippling brushes are expensive and used only for selected techniques. But you can achieve similar results by substituting two inexpensive 6-inch-wide chip brushes

bound together with painter's tape. Along with the how-tos featured in Part 3 of this book, you'll find some suggested substitutions and modifications you can make in place of more expensive tools.

In addition to paint and tools for the decorative paint treatments you're planning, be sure you have enough preparation supplies—including drop cloths, plastic sheeting, primer, and painter's tape—to get your space ready for decorative painting. See page 32 for room preparation details.

Estimating

A successful decorative painting project requires good planning. Accurate estimates of the amount of materials you need, the amount of time a project will take, and the amount of money the whole thing will cost ensure optimal results.

Paint Quantities

Before you go to the home center or paint store, take measurements of all the surfaces you plan to paint, and determine the area of these surfaces in square feet.

To find the wall area of a room, add the wall lengths to find the perimeter length; then multiply the perimeter length by the wall height. Subtract the area of any windows, doors, or other areas that will not be painted. You can estimate 15 square feet for each standard window and 21 square feet for each standard door.

To find the area of a ceiling or floor, multiply the room width by the room length.

To estimate the number of gallons of regular paint you need for one coat, divide the total area to be painted by 300—the number of square feet a gallon of paint will cover. (Some paint labels say that coverage is 400 square feet per gallon, but 300 is a safer number to use for an estimate.)

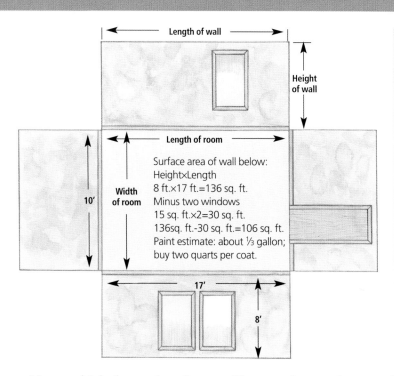

Length of wall

Height of wall

Length of room

Width of room

10'

Surface area of wall below:
Height×Length
8 ft.×17 ft.=136 sq. ft.
Minus two windows
15 sq. ft.×2=30 sq. ft.
136sq. ft.-30 sq. ft.=106 sq. ft.
Paint estimate: about ⅓ gallon;
buy two quarts per coat.

17'

8'

ESTIMATING PAINT
To estimate how much paint you'llneed, calculate thea rea of the surface you will be painting. For walls, multiply height times length. Deduct about 21 square feet for a standard door, 15 square feet for a standard window. To calculate the area of a flat ceiling, multiply the length of the room times the width. Figure that a gallon of paint will cover about 300 square feet.

Next, multiply the number of gallons by the number of coats you plan to paint. Most base coats require two coats of paint. Take into account that some surfaces, such as new drywall and plaster, soak up more paint than previously painted walls or paneling. When in doubt, round up; you'll be glad you have the extra paint if you need to do some touch-ups later on or if you decide to paint other surfaces in your room or home.

Glaze applied on its own covers approximately 300 square feet per gallon. However, the amount of glaze you actually use depends on the specific technique you select. Some techniques, like ragging off, use more glaze per square foot, because you apply large amounts of glaze to a surface and then remove it; other techniques require mixing a small amount of glaze with water and paint, so you might be able to cover 600 or more square feet of surface with one gallon of glaze. As with paint, round the quantity up when in doubt.

Time

A thorough paint job, as well as applying most decorative paint treatments, takes considerable time.

There aren't many shortcuts if you want to get good final results. You need to allow time for paint to dry between coats. Recommended drying times vary among paint brands, but generally, a coat of paint needs four to six hours of drying time.

Most decorative treatments in this book require a painted base coat with one or more layers of paint or glaze applied as a top coat. In general you'll need more than one day to complete most treatments. A typical painting plan might look like this:

Day 1: Prepare the room for painting (see page 32) and apply the first coat. If you start early enough on the first day, you may be able to apply a second coat of your base-coat paint.

Day 2: Apply a second coat of base-coat paint, if necessary. Prepare the room for decorative paint treatment, apply the decorative paint treatment, and then move back into the room. To save some time actually applying the decorative paint treatment, practice ahead on sample boards. For instructions on how to make sample boards, turn to page 41.

Budget

Decorative paint treatments require

high-quality paints, and price is a good indicator of quality. Paint that is durable, appears truer in color, and covers well typically costs $20 to $35 a gallon, depending on the brand you select. Glazes and other specialty paint products vary widely in cost, but in general, glazes cost $30 to $40 a gallon.

You can—but don't have to—spend a small fortune on specialty decorative paint tools. If you have limited funds, spend your money on tools that you'll use for a variety of techniques and applications, such as a high-quality trim brush, a 5-inch general coverage brush, roller frames, or a sea sponge. Be careful when purchasing cloths—cheesecloth, chamois, rags, and the like. Cloths should not shed or disintegrate during use. For more specific tool recommendations, turn to page 132.

While expensive compared with owning and using a tool for several years, disposable painting tools, such as foam rollers, plastic roller trays, and paper drop cloths, reduce tedious cleanup and can be an ideal choice for the do-it-yourself decorative painter.

SELECTING COLORS AND COLOR COMBINATIONS

Few decorating choices are more intimidating than selecting colors for a painting project. Here are some simple design tips and terms to help you choose the colors for your project.

The Color Wheel

The color wheel organizes color choices into 12 categories, or pure colors. The wheel is built on three groups of colors:
- Primary colors. Red, yellow, and blue are the primaries, the basis for all colors. They are equally spaced around the wheel and cannot be created by mixing any other colors.
- Secondary colors. Orange (equal parts yellow and red), purple (red and blue), and green (blue and yellow) are equally spaced between the primary colors.

- Tertiary colors. Mixing the primary colors with an equal amount of their nearest secondary colors gives six pure colors: red-orange, red-violet, yellow-orange, yellow-green, blue-green, and blue-violet.

Tones, Shades, Tints

For a decorative painting project, you probably won't use any of the 12 pure color-wheel colors because they are too intense. The colors used in decorating combine a pure color with white, black, or both white and black.
- Color + white produces a *tint*, which is a lighter *value* of the pure color. Tints appear closer to the center on the color wheel.
- Color + black produces a *shade*, which is darker value of the pure color. Shades appear on the outer rings of the color wheel.

- Color + black and white produces a *tone*, which is a muted or grayed-down pure color. Tones don't appear on most color wheels, but they are what you usually see featured in store paint displays.

Using the Color Wheel for Various Effects

Use the color wheel and some basic geometry to pick the color scheme for a project.

Monochromatic color schemes are created with the tints and shades of a single color.

Analogous color schemes combine colors that are next to or nearly next to one another on the color wheel.

Complementary color schemes pair colors that are directly opposite one another on the color wheel.

MATCH YOUR COLOR

Don't forget about color-matching services available at most paint stores and home centers. If you can't seem to find a color that works with a picture, accessory, or piece of fabric, have the item color-matched by computer. The resulting paint will be identical to at least one item in the room.

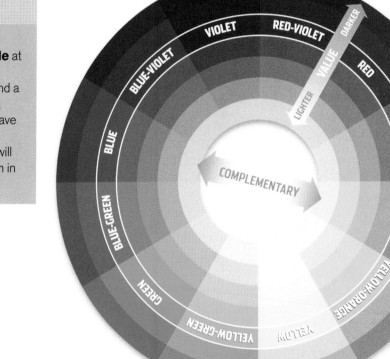

ANALOGOUS COLORS
Relying on an analogous color scheme of blues and greens, this room has a cool, soothing feeling, even though its furnishings are modern and graphic.

MONOCHROMATIC SCHEME
Monochromatic color schemes aren't boring when you vary the textures, tones, and patterns. In this living room, golden beiges appear in multiple tones in the diamond wall treatment, as well as in the fireplace stones, upholstery, and flooring.

COMPLEMENTARY COLORS
Combining complementary colors in a room—such as cherry red and sea green in this entryway—gives the room vibrancy and energy. Also, each color appears more intense when paired with its complement.

Even if you know what colors and decorative techniques you're going to use, deciphering the language of paint can be a challenge. Here are the basic terms you need to know to make the best choices for your projects.

Latex or Oil?

Latex (water-base) paints are the most commonly available paints now. Almost any decorative technique can be accomplished—with excellent results—using latex paint. Latex paints have the advantage of being easy to work with, easy to clean up, and quick-drying. Wastes and used rags pose little hazard too. The techniques in this book rely almost exclusively on latex paints and glazes.

Alkyds or oil-base paints provide better coverage and can cling to a wider range of surfaces, especially difficult surfaces, such as plastic or metal. Some decorative painters use oil-base paints because they take longer to dry, allowing more time to work with the paint and glaze to develop the decorative effect. (Extender additives are available for latex paints if the drying time is too short.) Alkyds require solvents, such as paint thinner, to clean up. Residues of oil-base paint and rags used with them are more hazardous than those of water-base paint.

Sheen

Depending on the paint brand you buy, you'll have three to five sheens, or levels of shininess, to choose from. The photos on these pages show the relative reflectivity of various sheen options. Some sheens suit certain applications better than others:

■ **Flat:** Muted appearance. Good finish for walls and ceilings. Not recommended for high-use surfaces or as a base coat for decorative painting techniques.

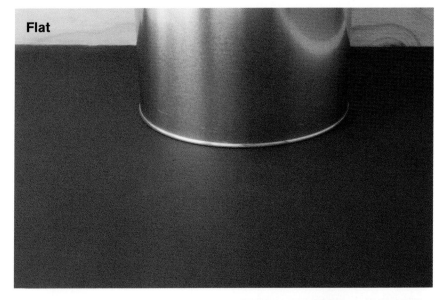

Flat

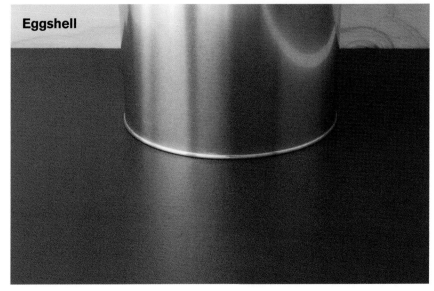

Eggshell

■ **Eggshell:** Muted appearance. Resists dirt better than flat paint. Good for walls and ceilings and other low- to mid-use surfaces. Not recommended for high-use surfaces or as a base coat for decorative painting.

■ **Satin:** Richer appearance. Resists dirt and oil better than flat. Good for walls and ceilings, including those that require occasional cleaning.

■ **Semigloss:** Slightly shiny appearance. Good for high-use walls and all woodwork, doors, and furniture.

■ **Gloss:** Shiny, almost reflective, appearance. Water-resistant. Good for trim, doors, cabinets, and furniture.

Glazes

Glazes can be applied by themselves or mixed with solid paint to create a tinted, translucent liquid. Glazes are crucial to giving decorative paint projects depth and richness. They also make latex paint easier to work with by providing additional drying time. Most glazes appear milky when first opened, but will dry to clear or semitransparent. Glazes are generally

Satin

Semigloss

Gloss

neutral and can be mixed with any color paint.

Glazes offer a wide array of shimmering effects: opalescent, metallic, pearlized, and more. You may need to experiment with several glazes until you find the right effect for your project. Pretinted glazes are also available in many popular decorating colors, including green, blue, brown, cream, and rusty red. You don't always need to purchase tinted glazes, but one may be an appropriate choice for your project or desired effect.

There are few shortcuts to doing a painting job both well and quickly. But if you do the job right the first time—even if it takes longer than you'd like—you'll save time by not having to go back and fix mistakes or redo parts later on. Preparing the painting area carefully by following these hints will help make the actual painting go as smoothly as possible.

Clean Starts

Paint should be applied to relentlessly clean surfaces. While most walls require only a good wiping with a slightly moist rag, kitchen and bathroom walls should be thoroughly scrubbed down. Use cleaning agents or degreasers if necessary. Tackle any stains—whether created by messy hands or the results of mold or moisture damage—before starting a paint project. See page 148.

Making Repairs

Cracks and holes should be repaired, filled, sanded, and allowed to completely dry before painting. Most spackling products dry in 30 minutes or less, so be sure that your repairs are ready to be painted. Turn to page 144 for more about patching wall holes.

Taping and Covering

Taping is time-consuming work, but doing a good job enables you to paint faster, spend less time on touch-ups, and achieve a sharper, cleaner edge on your finished work. Rely on painter's tape, not masking tape, for your painting projects—it makes sharper lines and pulls off better. The tape area of the home center or paint store offers many convenient products, such as premade adhesive corners for windows, adhesive baseboard protectors, and tape applicators.

Quick Fixes

Before you start painting, have supplies close at hand to deal with drips and spills. A few wet rags, a small bucket of mildly sudsy water, and a roll of paper towels will handle most minor paint mishaps.

PROTECT FLOORS
Cover the floor completely to keep the inevitable dri and splashes off. Merely covering the floor with loos drop cloths is a sure invitation to having an area uncovered at just the wrong time.

START WITH A CLEAN SURFACE
Paint sticks better to clean surfaces. Wash handprints and stains off walls to prevent them from showing through the new paint.

SURFACE REPAIR
Drive in popped nails or screws and fill and sand all holes and cracks before rolling on base-coat paint.

DECORATIVE PAINTING CHECKLIST

For fantastic decorative painting results, make sure you do the following:

- Select a room, wall, or surface for decorative painting.

- Choose decorative paint technique(s) appropriate for the surface.

- Research the tools, materials, and skills needed to accomplish the technique.

- Estimate the area of the space you'll be painting.

- Plan for enough time to complete the technique. Allow for adequate drying time.

- Select the number and types of colors needed for the treatment.

- Learn or test the technique on a sample board.

- Remove as much furniture from the room as possible.

- Fill the room with adequate light. Bring in additional lamps if necessary.

- Clean and dust all surfaces to be painted.

- Cover floors with drop cloths.

- Remove electrical outlet covers.

- Drape plastic, fabric, or paper sheeting over any furniture that's still in the room.

- Dress in clothing appropriate for painting.

- Organize your plan—which surfaces you'll work on first, second, and third.

- Tape around all windows, doors, trim, and floors where they meet the walls.

- Prime/paint walls with base coat color.

GOOF-PROOF WITH TAPE
Apply painter's tape to trim, decorative molding, baseboards, and window and door frames to maintain a crisp edge and minimize cleanup.

Decorative
PAINTING TECHNIQUES

Here are 36 decorative painting techniques with all the step-by-step instructions, material lists, and how-to details you need to get the job done right.

The techniques are grouped according to the skills and tools you need.

■ **PAGES 36–69** focus on applicator-based techniques. These classic, versatile techniques are good places to start if you've never tackled a decorative painting project before. You'll learn essential movements and hand and wrist positioning, as well as how to work with basic decorative painting tools such as sponges, rags, rollers, combs, and specialty brushes.

■ **PAGES 70–77** cover antiquing techniques. You'll learn several ways to give new items the appearance of well-worn heirlooms in just a few hours.

■ **PAGES 78–99** are dedicated to some of the most powerful decorative painting techniques—those that create the appearance of other, often expensive, materials. Find out how to create the illusion of leather, marble, and more in this section.

■ **PAGES 100–115** showcase dynamic treatments such as stenciling, taping, and stamping, as well as working with eye-catching metallic paints and leaf.

■ **PAGES 116–129** show how to produce richly textured treatments by combining paint and glaze with plaster and other additives.

MAKE THE RIGHT MOVES

Throughout this section, you'll find motion-capture images that highlight key aspects of a technique's movement or position. Pay special attention to descriptions and depictions of fingers, hands, wrists, arms, and even the body.

STANDARD TOOLS

You'll use some decorative painting tools, like this stippling brush, in dozens of different decorative paint treatments. For frequently used tools, purchase high-quality items that you can wash and reuse for multiple projects and techniques.

SPECIAL TOOLS

Specialty tools like this double roller are sometimes necessary to get the desired results. Throughout this section, you'll learn to separate the must-have decorative painting tools from the nonessentials.

Color washing is a basic and essential decorative painting technique. Most decorative painting techniques rely on your ability to apply paint and paint/glaze combinations to a surface and then to work the paint to achieve a desired effect. This is exactly what's involved in color washing.

The color-wash technique described on pages 36 through 41 shows you how to apply one, two, or three layers of glaze to a base-coated wall and how to work in additional glazes for increasingly richer effects. Although these pages showcase working with one, two, and three glazes, you can color wash with as many glazes as you desire, depending on your supplies and decorating needs.

YOU'LL NEED

TIME: Half to one day to cover a 400-square-foot area.

SKILLS: Mixing glazes, rolling on glaze, working with glaze, positioning and repositioning cloth pom-poms.

TOOLS: Rubber gloves, foam roller (one for each color applied), roller tray (one for each color applied), soft rags or cheesecloth, stippling brush or two wide chip brushes, soft blending brush.

MATERIALS: Light yellow latex base coat; deep bronze, brown, and sage green latex paints; latex glaze.

APPLY ONE GLAZE.

Because it's one of the easiest, most forgiving, and most versatile decorative painting techniques, color washing is a great treatment for beginning painters. Here, a golden glaze atop a yellow base coat creates a sunny, soft look.

1 APPLY GLAZE.

Apply base-coat paint and let dry. In a plastic container, mix one part glaze, one part paint, and one part water; stir until blended. Pour glaze mixture into a small roller tray. Load a foam roller with the glaze and roll off excess. Holding the roller with a loose and flexible wrist, roll on glaze in a series of intersecting, random bands. Overlap some passes and leave some areas unglazed. Apply glaze to an area about 3×3 feet, leaving uneven edges.

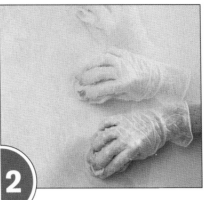

2 BLEND AND THIN GLAZE.

Wearing rubber gloves, grasp a piece of soft cotton cloth or cheesecloth in a loose pom-pom shape (for more on forming cloth pom-poms, see page 49). Pat the cloth along the edges of the glaze bands, pushing glaze onto the unglazed portion of the surface. Continually rotate your wrist and move your entire hand along on the edges, blending and thinning the glaze as you go.

3 MAINTAIN A CLEAN RAG.

When your rag becomes laden with glaze and paint, rearrange the cloth to find a clean area. Create a new pom-pom and continue pouncing the wet edges of the glaze. Rearrange your rag when it begins applying glaze to the wall rather than moving glaze around.

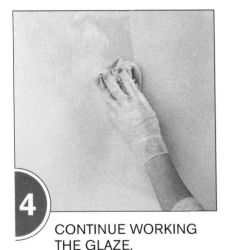

4 CONTINUE WORKING THE GLAZE.

Pounce within the bands of applied glaze, rotating your wrist continually. Work the glaze to create subtle highlights (areas with less glaze) and shadows (areas with more glaze). Continue repositioning the cloth to use clean portions of the rag. When all areas of the rag are glaze-laden, soak the rag in lightly soapy water and begin using a new cloth.

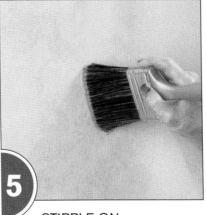

5 STIPPLE ON MORE TEXTURE.

Before the glaze dries, tap fast and frequently along the blended lines of glaze with a stippling brush or a pair of wide chip brushes that you secure together with painter's tape. Tap with the end bristles of the brush straight down on the glaze and try to soften any remaining lines.

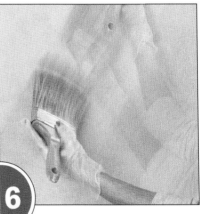

6 SOFTEN THE TEXTURE.

With the glaze still slightly wet, brush over the entire treated surface with a soft, broad brush, using a crisscross motion. Brush very lightly and use the tips of the brush to soften any remaining harder edges of glaze. Reposition yourself at another section of the wall and repeat the application process, feathering in your new work with the old.

Color washing with one, two, or three colors *(continued)*

PICKING COLORS

The effect of color washing varies significantly depending on the number and intensity of colors you choose to work with on the top coat. Try color washing a glaze that is two shades lighter than the base coat. Or use a pair of top-coat shades: one two shades lighter, the other two shades darker. You also can mix in other colors, depending on your color scheme and decorating goals. Pair warm-toned grays and browns with a scheme that relies on reds, oranges, or yellows. Pair cool-toned grays and neutrals with blues, greens, or violets.

MIX TWO GLAZES.

A two-color wash is an easy way to create a custom wall treatment that incorporates two different hues that may be present in the furniture, fabrics, and accessories in a room. Here, light and dark gold glazes are applied over a yellow base coat.

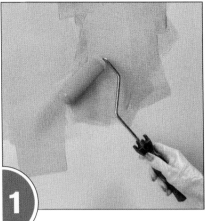

1 APPLY TWO GLAZE COLORS.

Begin with a base-coated wall. Mix the two glazes (one part glaze, one part paint, and one part water) in two separate plastic containers. Pour the glaze mixtures into two roller trays. Load the first foam roller with glaze and roll onto the surface with loose, overlapping movements. While the first glaze color is still wet, roll the second glaze color on top and around the first color in a series of random intersecting bands. Allow some portions of the surface to remain unglazed. Apply the glazes over a 3×3-foot area, leaving uneven edges.

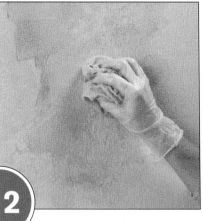

2 BLEND THE GLAZES.

Form a loose pom-pom of soft cloth or cheesecloth in your hand. Pounce the edges of the applied glaze with the pom-pom, blending and softening the edges. Rotate your wrist and reposition your arm frequently, following the rolled-on application of the glaze. Try to push and thin the glaze onto the unglazed portions of the surface.

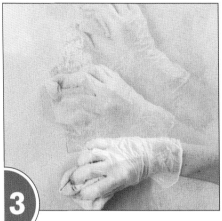

3 KEEP THE RAG CLEAN.

Using a fresh portion of the rag, blend glaze-heavy areas with areas where the two glazes meet. Allow glazes to blend and mix in some places; allow individual glazes to remain unmixed in a few areas as well. As the pom-pom fills with glaze, reposition the cloth and use clean portions of the rag. When all areas of the rag are glaze-laden, soak the rag in lightly soapy water and use a new cloth.

4 STIPPLE FOR ADDITIONAL TEXTURE.

While the glazes are still wet, use a stippling brush or taped-together chip brushes to tap and subtly blend the glazes. The tapping motion is straight and direct; only the ends of the bristles hit the glaze. After stippling, brush over the entire treated surface with a wide, soft brush.

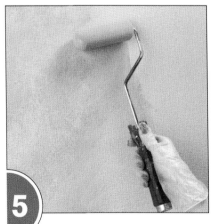

5 MOVE TO A NEW AREA.

Apply the first and then the second glazes with foam rollers, slightly overlapping new random bands of glaze with the finished section. Continue using the cloth pom-pom, stippling brush, and soft blending brush to work the glazes.

KEEP A WET EDGE

The key to color-washing success is to keep the surface and edges wet as you pounce on the glaze with the cloth, working and blending the colors. Have a spray bottle of water on hand and lightly mist any color-washed area that you need to continue working on for a few minutes more.

Color washing with one, two, or three colors *(continued)*

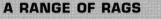

A RANGE OF RAGS

The type and quality of rags used for decorative painting can affect how a treatment turns out. Coarser cloths (such as mesh netting and polyester or cotton-poly cheesecloths) yield more distinct texture; finer cloths (chamois, cotton jersey, and sheeting) result in softer, subtler effects. Avoid cloths that shed fibers as you use them. Machine washing and drying rags before you first use them can eliminate excess fibers. Always experiment with a new rag on a sample board to ensure that it leaves a clean, fiber-free finish.

COMBINE THREE GLAZES

This three-color version of the color-wash technique uses light and dark gold on top of a light yellow base coat. Patches of purple glaze have been applied in small quantities to serve as an accent.

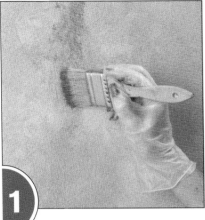

1 APPLY THREE TOP-COAT GLAZES.

Begin with a base-coated wall. In separate containers mix one part glaze, one part paint, and one part water for each glaze mixture. Pour the glaze mixtures into three trays. Load foam rollers with the first and second glazes and roll onto the surface with loose, overlapping movements. Using a third foam roller or a chip brush, apply the third glaze color in short, narrow bands on top of the other two glazes. Allow some wall to remain untouched by any of the three glazes. Work in areas of about 3×3 feet.

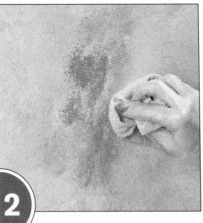

2 POUNCE FOR TEXTURE.

Using a loose pom-pom of soft cloth or cheesecloth, pounce and blend edges of the glaze. Rotate your wrist and change your arm position frequently. Follow the lines of glaze application, and work the glaze farther out, blending the glaze with surrounding glaze. Push some glaze into unglazed areas of the surface.

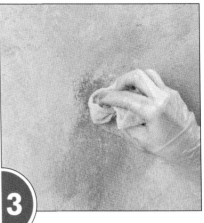

3 BLEND THE GLAZES.

Pay attention to areas where all three glaze colors meet. Allow one glaze to dominate these areas, blending the other two more thoroughly. Rotate your wrist and rearrange your cloth frequently to ensure that you don't muddy the surface by applying mixed glazes from previous pounces.

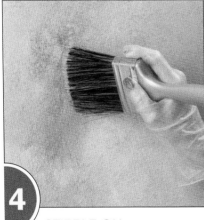

4 STIPPLE ON MORE TEXTURE.

Tap the still-wet glazes with a stippling brush or taped-together chip brushes to further blend the glazes. Tap perpendicular to the glaze. Brush over the entire treated surface with a wide, soft brush.

5 MOVE TO A NEW AREA.

Move on to the next portion of the surface, rolling on the first two glazes and brushing on the third glaze, allowing all glazes to overlap each other. Continue blending with the cloth pom-pom, stippling brush, and a soft blending blush.

SAMPLE BOARDS

Sample boards help you figure out what colors and techniques you should use for your treatments. They also let you practice and refine your technique before working with an actual surface. To make sample boards, cut a 4x8-foot sheet of ⅛-inch hardboard into eight 2x2-foot pieces. If you don't have a table saw or circular saw, you can have the board cut to size in the lumber area of a home center. Prime the sample boards and allow them to dry. Then, try out new techniques or color combinations on the sample boards until you're satisfied with the results. You can paint over old tests to reuse the boards.

GRADING AND GRADUATED COLOR BLENDS

This soft and serene wall treatment is both simple to create and stunning to behold. The effect looks best when you work with an assortment of colors that have similar color bases or intensities. Use four or five colors that appear on the same paint deck strip—or select colors from neighboring paint deck strips at approximately the same position on the strip.

YOU'LL NEED

TIME: Half to one day to cover a 400-square-foot area.

SKILLS: Selecting paint colors, blending paint, painting with consistent, long strokes.

TOOLS: Trim brush, 4- to 6-inch-wide brush, tape measure, pencil, carpenter's level.

MATERIALS: Four or five similar colors of latex paint.

CHOOSE GOOD BRUSHES

You'll use a few brushes over and over again in your decorative painting projects. The best brushes have wooden handles that fit comfortably in your hand. Check that the metal band that holds the bristles in place (the ferrule) is stainless steel or another non-rusting metal. The bristles should taper down to form an even edge, even when you press the brush against a flat surface. Play with the bristles a bit; they should feel flexible and springy and have split ends (to better hold paint).

BLEND BANDS OF COLOR.

Four shades of cool blue-green in this bathroom cascade in roughly equal horizontal bands that blend gently from darkest, at the bottom of the wall, to lightest at the top portion.

1 MEASURE AND MARK.

Before painting, measure and mark 2-foot-wide horizontal bands to serve as references. Use a carpenter's level and a pencil to draw light, level lines. Starting at the top edge of the wall, use a trim brush to apply the lightest paint color along the ceiling line.

2 BRUSH ON FIRST COLOR.

After the ceiling line is painted, use a wider brush to continue applying the light color to the topmost section of the wall. Brush on paint in long, horizontal movements, using the pencil line as a guide. Blend in strokes with a light feathering motion, first touching the loaded brush to the wet paint and then gradually applying more pressure and paint as you go farther into the movement. Fill in the entire marked portion of the wall with paint.

3 BLEND IN SECOND COLOR.

Using a new brush—or after thoroughly cleaning and rinsing the wide brush you've already used—brush on the next darker color in the second 2-foot-wide band. Work the darker paint color up into the lighter color with sweeping horizontal motions. Brush back over areas you've already painted to further mix the two paint colors. Blend the darker color up several inches into the lighter section above.

4 BLEND ADDITIONAL COLORS.

Continue brushing on darker paint colors in each of the lower sections. Use a new or cleaned brush for each new paint color. For a consistent effect, always work the darker, lower color up and into the lighter color, extending the color blend up several inches into the section above.

SPONGING ON

Sponging on was one of the first decorative painting techniques to gain mass appeal. Even today, sponging on is one of the first techniques that new painters try. The benefits of the technique are obvious: Sponging provides quick texture for almost any painted surface. The tools and materials are inexpensive and easy to work with.

Although sponging on high-contrast paint colors and using a heavy-handed technique have fallen out of popularity, you can easily modify the technique to produce striking and more subtle effects. The key to softening sponged-on looks is adding equal parts glaze and water to the top-coat paints, creating a semi-translucent layer of color.

YOU'LL NEED

TIME: Half to one day to cover a 400-square-foot area.

SKILLS: Selecting paints, mixing glazes and paints, applying paint with a sponge.

TOOLS: Sea sponges, mixing containers, paint tray, bucket of clean water.

MATERIALS: Light-color base coat of latex paint, two medium-color latex paints for top coat, glaze.

SPONGE ON TEXTURE.

For a fresh take on the classic technique of sponging on, combine glaze with two medium-toned latex paints and then apply it atop a light base coat.

1. LOAD SPONGE.

Apply base-coat paint to surface and let dry. In two plastic containers, mix one part glaze, one part paint, and one part water; stir until blended. Pour one glaze mixture into a roller tray. Moisten the sea sponge in a bucket of clean water. If the sponge is new, work the sponge several times until it becomes loose and pliable. Wearing rubber gloves, dip the sponge into the glaze, covering an area on it approximately 2 inches square. Blot off excess glaze on the upper portion of the tray or on a separate plastic plate.

2. DAB ON GLAZE.

Starting in an upper corner (or other logical starting point), dab the sponge on the wall lightly. Lift your hand, rotate your wrist, and slightly reposition your arm. Dab lightly again. Continue this motion, creating an ever-larger area of applied glaze. Use different parts of the sponge to dab against the wall so that the pores of the sponge don't become overly consistent and obvious. Refill and blot your sponge whenever your dabbing stops making an obvious mark.

3. WORK IN TIGHT AREAS.

When sponging on glaze in a corner or other tight area, tear off a small piece of sponge, approximately 2 inches square, and use the smaller piece to dab on glaze. Use the same motion to apply glaze with the smaller sponge.

4. EVALUATE YOUR WORK.

After you sponge on a 3-foot-square section of glaze, step back 8 to 10 feet and survey the overall texture and consistency of your sponging. You should not be able to discern any distinct edges or pores from the sponge. For areas where glaze appears too heavy, dab with a clean, slightly moist sponge to remove some glaze. For areas where too much base-coat color shows through, sponge on additional glaze.

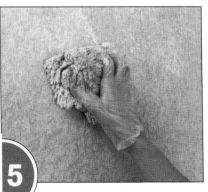

5. ADD THE OTHER GLAZE.

With a new or thoroughly cleaned sponge, begin sponging on a second glaze color to the top coat. Use the second glaze color as more of an accent, dabbing the sponge more lightly and allowing more space between sponge impressions. Continue to rotate the wrist, reposition your arm, and use different portions of the sponge to dab against the wall. Refill and blot the sponge whenever you stop leaving noticeable impressions.

UPDATING A CLASSIC

Sponging on can look garish if the colors are too deep or contrast too much. The keys to sponging on a treatment that will look fresh and modern are taking your time, selecting appropriate top-coat colors (those that are two or three shades lighter or darker than your base coat), and mixing glaze and water with your top-coat paints for additional depth and luminance.

SPONGING OFF

Sponging off uses the same tools and motion as sponging on, but with sponging off, the focus is on removing, not applying, paint and glaze. Sponging off produces a subtle, soft effect that adds depth and visual interest to an otherwise flat surface. The technique enables you to work in other hues that may be lacking in the initial base-coat color—more yellow, green, or red are common changes.

Sponging off can also be a great fix for an initial wall color that is close to what you want, but not quite. By sponging off a lighter or darker glaze, you can adjust the appearance of the base-coat color to meet your decorating goals.

YOU'LL NEED

TIME: Half a day to apply treatment to 400-square-foot area.

SKILLS: Tinting glazes, rolling on glaze, working glaze with sponge.

TOOLS: Mixing containers, roller tray, foam or cloth roller, extension rod, sea sponges, bucket of clean water.

MATERIALS: Darker-color base coat of latex paint, light-color latex paints for top coat, glaze.

SPONGE OFF GLAZE.

Give a light-color wall a boost of color and drama by rolling on a coat of darker glaze and then sponging it off for texture and interest.

1 ROLL ON TOP-COAT GLAZE.

Paint the base color on the surface and let dry. In a plastic container, mix two parts glaze, one part paint, and one part water; stir until blended. Pour glaze into roller tray. Load roller with glaze and roll off excess on tray. Roll on a small section of darker glaze in a "W" pattern and finish off with consistent vertical roller strokes.

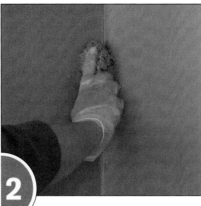

2 APPLY GLAZE TO TIGHT SPACES.

Tear off a small piece of sea sponge or use a corner paint pad. Dip the sponge or pad into the glaze and wipe on glaze in corners and other small areas where the roller can't fit.

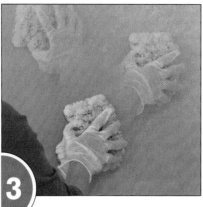

3 REMOVE SOME GLAZE.

While the rolled-on glaze is still wet, press a clean, slightly moist sea sponge into the glaze, removing some of the glaze and revealing the base-coat color underneath. Lift your hand, rotate your wrist, and slightly reposition your arm. Press into glaze again. Continue removing glaze, creating a larger area. Change the portion of the sponge that you press into the glaze so no area of the sponge becomes oversaturated with glaze.

4 CLEAN SPONGE.

When the sponge is no longer removing glaze, rinse out the sponge in a bucket of water. Wring out the water from the sponge and continue sponging off glaze. After rinsing two or three sponges' worth of glaze, change the water in the bucket.

SPONGED LOOKS: LIGHTER OR DARKER

Whether you're sponging on glaze or sponging off glaze, the glaze color you're working with can be either lighter or darker than the base coat. There aren't any right color combinations here, but the shade difference between the base coat and top coat can produce dramatically different results:

Light peach base coat

Sponged-on medium orange glaze

Sponged-on light yellow glaze

These examples start with the same solid base coat. A lighter glaze and paint mixture was sponged onto the first example. A darker glaze was sponged onto he second example.

Medium green base coat

Sponged-off darker green glaze

Sponged-off lighter green glaze

The starting point here is a solid medium-green base coat. A darker glaze was rolled on and then sponged off in the first example. A lighter glaze was rolled on and sponged off for the second example.

RAGGING ON

The process of ragging on is similar to sponging on in many ways. Both techniques give surfaces texture and visual interest by adding a layer of paint and glaze atop a painted base coat. However, ragging on gives you more opportunity than sponging on to experiment with and control the texture of the glaze you add to the surface. The way you hold the rag—in addition to the fiber type, weave, size, and edges of the cloth—affects the final outcome of the treatment.

RAG ON GLAZE.

Deep blue walls could have been overwhelming. A ragged-on finish of light blue glaze allows the walls to keep their mellow hue, but lowers the intensity.

RAG VARIETY

You can use various types of rags for ragging on or off. However, for consistency, always use the same type and size of rag when you apply a technique to a surface.

RAGGED LOOKS: LIGHTER OR DARKER

Just as with sponging on and off (see pages 44–47), the relationship between top-coat glaze color and the solid base-coat color can create vastly different effects when ragging on and off. Experiment on sample boards (see page 41) with lighter and darker glazes before selecting the color combination to use on an entire wall or room.

| Medium blue base coat | Ragged-on medium gray-blue glaze | Ragged-on light gray-blue glaze |

Starting with a solid blue base coat, a darker glaze was applied with a rag mitt for the first example. A lighter glaze was ragged on with the same kind of mitt for the second example.

| Light purple base coat | Ragged-off deep pink glaze | Ragged-off white glaze |

Starting with a solid purple base coat, a darker glaze was rolled on and then ragged off for the first example. A lighter glaze was rolled on and then ragged off for the second example.

1. RAG ON TEXTURE.

To rag on a finish with greater contrast and more distinct lines and grain, hold your cloth in a *wrinkled pom-pom arrangement*. Grab an unfolded rag with one hand and bring your fingers together in a light fist. Your rag will have numerous and obvious folds.

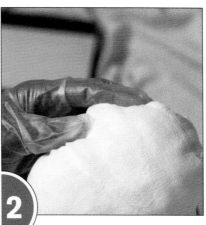

2. RAG ON SMOOTHLY.

To rag on a finish with more consistent texture and fewer lines and edges, hold your cloth in a *smooth pom-pom* arrangement. Use two hands to shape the rag into a round ball. Smooth out any wrinkles and hold the pom-pom in one hand. Tuck in or under all the tails of cloth, creating a smooth, round bundle of fabric.

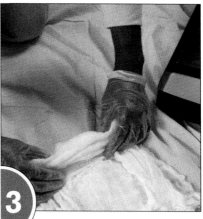

3. RAG ROLL.

To roll on a finish with distinct edges and a linear effect, roll fabric into a tubular shape. Tie each end of the roll with thin cotton string to maintain the rolled shape, if desired. Roll the fabric through glaze poured into a roller tray and then onto the base-coated surface. Roll in diagonal, overlapping passes for best effect.

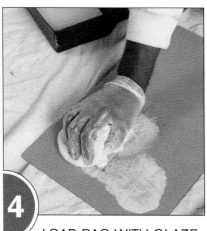

4. LOAD RAG WITH GLAZE.

Apply base-coat paint to surface and let dry. In a plastic container, mix one part glaze, one part paint, and one part water; stir until blended. Pour glaze mixture into a small tray. Wearing rubber gloves, dip the cloth pom-pom into glaze and blot off the excess on the upper portion of the tray or a separate plastic plate.

5. DAB ON GLAZE.

Press the cloth and glaze onto the surface. Rotate your wrist and slightly reposition your arm. Press the cloth onto the surface again. When pressing the cloth onto the wall no longer applies glaze, reload your cloth with glaze, blot off the excess, and continue pressing and repositioning the cloth as before.

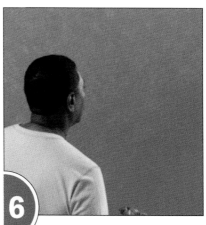

6. EVALUATE YOUR WORK.

After you complete a section approximately 3 feet square, step back 8 to 10 feet and evaluate the texture and consistency of your treatment. While the glaze is still wet, press a clean, slightly moist cloth onto areas where glaze appears too thick; press a rag loaded with glaze onto areas where glaze appears too thin. Soften unwanted lines or edges by pressing a wet, clean cloth into the glaze.

RAGGING OFF

Ragging off, like its companion decorative painting technique of ragging on, gives you significant opportunity to experiment and customize the texture and consistency of the glaze that appears on the wall. The way you hold the rag and the type of rag you use both affect the look of your final finish. Like other subtractive techniques (see sidebar on the opposite page), ragging off requires you to use—and then remove—a larger quantity of paint or glaze than you would for most additive techniques. Round up materials estimates and purchase supplies accordingly when preparing to apply subtractive treatments.

YOU'LL NEED

TIME: Half to one day to cover a 400-square-foot area.

SKILLS: Rolling on glaze, selecting glazes and paints.

TOOLS: Mixing containers, roller tray, foam or cloth roller, extension rod, cloth rags, bucket of clean water.

MATERIALS: Medium base coat of latex paint, darker-color latex paints for top coat, glaze.

RAG OFF GLAZE.

Applying a darker, contrasting top coat of glaze to a medium base coat of paint creates a richly textured appearance without the application of new plaster or drywall compound.

ROLL ON GLAZE TOP COAT.

Apply base-coat paint to the surface and let dry. In a plastic container mix two parts glaze, one part paint, and one part water; stir until blended. Pour glaze into roller tray. Load roller with glaze and roll off excess on tray. Roll on a small section of darker glaze in a "W" pattern and finish off with consistent vertical roller strokes.

REMOVE GLAZE TOP COAT.

Wearing rubber gloves, form a cloth rag into the desired shape (see page 49 for examples). While the glaze is still wet, dab the cloth onto the surface and lift off some of the glaze. Rotate your wrist, reposition your arm, and dab again, holding the cloth at a slightly different angle. When the cloth no longer removes glaze, reposition the cloth in your hand to expose clean portions. Continue dabbing and removing glaze. You might also experiment with using a wiping or rolling motion to remove glaze from the surface.

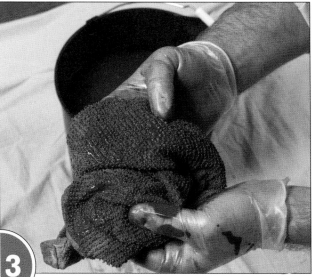

MAINTAIN A CLEAN RAG.

When the cloth no longer has clean portions and you find that you no longer can remove glaze from the surface when you press on it, wash the rag in a bucket of clean water, wringing the rag several times to remove as much glaze and water as possible. You can reuse rags after they dry.

OTHER TOOLS

Although cheesecloth is most commonly used for ragging on and off, you can do these techniques with linen, thin cotton cloth, old T-shirts, crumpled paper, plastic shopping bags, lint-free terry cloth, and even bubble wrap. Always test a new tool on a sample board before you apply it to an entire wall. Make sure you have enough of the selected applicator on hand before you begin a project.

ADDITIVE VS. SUBTRACTIVE

There are two types of decorative painting techniques. Additive techniques achieve their final look through the application of paint or other material to a surface. In subtractive techniques, you apply material to a surface, then remove some of it.

FROTTAGE

Frottage combines Old World texture with a soft yet contemporary attitude. Based on the French word *frotter*, meaning "to rub," this technique has numerous variations. The basic technique involves pressing a flat sheet (of paper, plastic, or fabric) into wet paint and then removing the sheet to produce a richly mottled surface. The consistency of the glaze you apply for the top coat and the type of sheeting material you choose both affect the final look of the treatment. For dramatic results use top- and base-coat colors that starkly contrast; for a more subtle effect, pair similar top-coat and base-coat colors.

YOU'LL NEED

TIME: Half to one day to cover a 400-square-foot area.

SKILLS: Rolling on glaze, applying paper or plastic sheeting to wall.

TOOLS: Newspaper or roll of kraft paper, container for mixing, roller tray, foam or cloth rollers.

MATERIALS: Light base coat of latex paint, medium-color latex paints for top coat, glaze.

APPLY RICH TEXTURE.

Frottage, applied here using newspaper to remove a darker top-coat glaze, gives walls a stately Old World flair in just a few minutes.

1 ROLL ON A COAT OF GLAZE.

Apply base-coat paint to the surface and let dry. In a plastic container mix one part glaze and one part paint; stir until blended. Pour the glaze into a roller tray. Load the roller with glaze and roll off excess on the tray. Start at a top corner (or other logical place), and roll on a section of glaze several inches larger than a sheet of newspaper or kraft paper. Roll on the glaze in long, vertical strokes.

2 APPLY A SHEET OF PAPER.

Using both hands, hold the top corners of a square of newspaper or kraft paper and position the paper so it's level. Press the paper onto the still-wet glaze. Brush palms down and around paper, until paper seems consistently attached to the wall.

3 REMOVE THE PAPER.

Curl up the top corners of the paper. With thumbs and index fingers, remove the paper from the wall in one smooth movement, revealing the texture underneath. Be careful that the glaze-coated paper avoids contact with the wall. Fold up the glaze-coated paper and dispose of it.

4 GLAZE AND APPLY PAPER AGAIN.

Using the same application technique, roll on glaze and apply second square of paper to wall. Allow the applied areas to overlap ¼ to ½ inch to create a blended, seamlike effect.

OR TRY THIS ...

Rather than use newspaper or large sheets of kraft paper to remove a glaze top coat, you can also do the frottage technique using 2-foot squares of clear or black plastic sheeting. Purchase plastic drop cloths, tarps, or even trash bags to use for this technique.

For an enhanced grid effect, cut pieces of plastic sheeting with a sharp utility knife into consistent squares. Mark a series of horizontal and vertical guidelines with a pencil, tape measure, and carpenter's level to help you keep your lines straight. See page 61 for more advice on measuring and marking off guidelines.

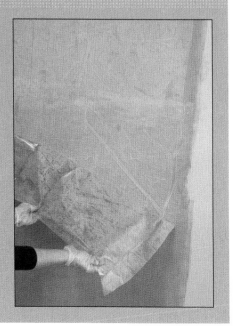

DOUBLE ROLLING

For years, professional decorative painters have produced richly mottled surfaces by rolling on and blending two colors of paint at the same time. Although you don't need to purchase a double roller and tray as shown here to execute this technique, these special tools make the process go twice as fast. Once difficult to find and expensively priced, double rollers, covers, and trays now are available at most home centers and paint stores at reasonable prices. As you shop for supplies for this treatment, explore the variety of textured roller covers available, including bilevel, long-nap, sculpted, and wire-loop varieties.

YOU'LL NEED

TIME: Half day to apply treatment to 400-square-foot area.

SKILLS: Double rolling, selecting paint colors.

TOOLS: Double roller, double roller covers, double roller tray, regular roller, regular roller tray, five-in-one tool.

MATERIALS: Two shades of latex paint, latex paint extender (optional).

ROLL AND BLEND TWO COLORS.

Two shades of gold, consistently double-rolled onto a wall, play off one another in this room, catching light in varying ways.

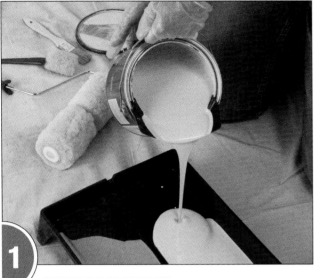

1 PREPARE THE TRAY.

Pour one color of latex paint into one side of a double tray. Pour the second color into the other. Be careful not to dribble paint into the opposite side. Load the double roller with both paints, carefully blotting off excess paint in the tray's grated area.

2 ROLL ON THE COLORS.

Begin rolling on paint to a primed wall, starting at an upper corner and working down and out. Roll on paint in random, overlapping passes. Apply paint randomly to a 4-foot-square section. You don't need to completely cover the wall with this application.

3 BLEND THE COLORS.

Using the same double roller, continue rolling over the wet section, using angled and overlapping strokes. Completely cover the section with paint. With each stroke, you blend colors further, so don't overwork the paints and end up overmixing them. Step back 8 to 10 feet and evaluate your technique. If the paint colors appear too distinct in some areas, roll lightly over these areas again. Move farther down the wall, working on a new 4-foot-square section.

4 CLEAN THE ROLLER.

After using the same double roller on three or four sections, clean excess and blended paint from the roller. Use a five-in-one tool or metal spackling knife to scrape off paint into a separate tray or container. Dispose of the scraped-off paint when you're done painting. Roll the double roller on brown kraft paper to remove additional paint, if desired.

Double rolling *(continued)*

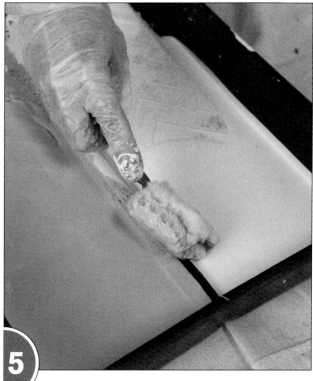

5 SPONGE ON IN TIGHT SPOTS.

To continue the double-rolling treatment into corners and other tight places, rip a 1- to 2-inch-diameter piece from a sea sponge or use a corner paint pad. (A special corner pad comes with some double-roller kits.) While wearing rubber gloves, dip half of the sponge or pad into one paint color; dip the other half into the other color. Blot the sponge or pad once or twice on a clean plastic plate or a piece of kraft paper.

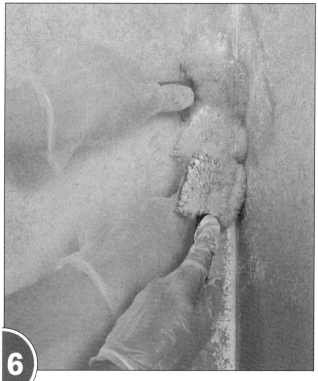

6 BLEND THE COLORS.

Dab the sponge or pad into a corner or tight area, starting high and working down. Lift your hand, rotate the tool, and dab the sponge or pad against the surface again. Continue rotating your hand, applying paint, and blending the two colors. Feather in the blended paint with the still-wet main sections.

GREAT COLOR COMBINATIONS

Selecting the paint colors for a double-rolling project can be a challenge. If the colors are too similar (for example, next to each other on the same paint strip), double rolling tends to overblend the colors into a muddled finish where neither original color is distinguishable and the texture is completely lost. If the colors contrast too much (rusty orange paired with sage green, for example), the colors tend to appear patchy, and the roller leaves distinct marks.

For best results, try to select colors that appear two positions apart from each other on the same paint strip or that appear at or near the same level on neighboring paint strips. For interesting texture and color contrast, the two top-coat paint colors should contrast slightly with the base coat. For a more subtle contrast, use the base-coat color as one of the two top-coat colors and avoid overblending the paint.

You can also apply top-coat paints with or without mixing in glaze. Adding glaze to the paints enhances color blending and increases the transparency of the top coat. As with any new decorative paint treatment or color combination, test on base-coated sample boards (see page 41 for more on sample boards).

COMBING: PINSTRIPES

Combing is a fun decorative technique that produces dynamic texture and—when executed with two contrasting paints—extreme color interest. For subtler effects, select two shades of color, or thin the top coat with additional glaze. Because the quality of the results of this technique depends on the consistent motion and pressure you apply, practice your technique and experiment with color and glaze combinations on sample boards before applying to the actual surface. Turn to page 41 for more information on sample boards.

YOU'LL NEED

TIME: Half to one day to apply treatment to 400-square-foot area, depending on the complexity of the design and the combination of techniques.

SKILLS: Rolling on paint, working with a utility knife, layering colors, combing through glazes.

TOOLS: Foam roller, roller tray, extension rod, rubber comb tool (or rubber squeegee and utility knife).

MATERIALS: Two shades of latex paint, latex paint extender (optional).

AN IDEAL ACCENT

Because combing often produces a bold, high-contrast look, you can use the technique in small but effective ways: as an accent on a cabinet door or tabletop, between taped-off stripes 12 to 18 inches wide on a wall, or on a portion of a wainscoted wall.

COMB GLAZE FOR CONTRAST.

Combing is a strong decorative painting choice if you want to showcase two different colors. Here, a bright green and soft cream paint are unmixed and provide distinct contrast.

Combing: Pinstripes *(continued)*

1 CHOOSE YOUR TOOL.

Purchase a rubber painting comb with desired teeth size and spacing. Or make your own comb by cutting notches into a 6- to 10-inch rubber squeegee with a sharp utility knife or scissors. Making your own combing tool enables you to cut notches to the size and spacing you desire.

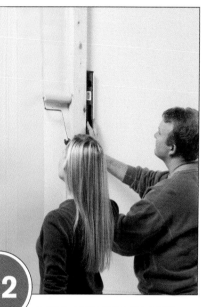

2 ROLL ON THE GLAZE.

Apply base-coat paint to the surface and let dry. In a plastic container, mix one part glaze, one part paint, and one part water; stir until blended. Pour the glaze mixture into a roller tray. Load a foam roller with glaze, blot off the excess on the tray, and then roll onto the wall. Start at an upper corner and roll down, applying the glaze in long vertical strokes. Continue applying glaze in a 12- to 18-inch band, all the way down to the baseboard or floor.

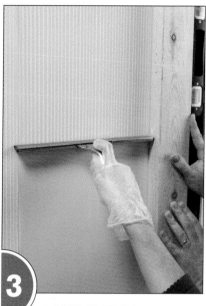

3 COMB THROUGH THE GLAZE.

Working quickly with the still-wet glaze, drag a rubber combing tool in one long, steady motion from the top of the wall to the bottom. Press the comb firmly against the surface to ensure consistent contact and crisp lines. Or for a more casual look, vary the speed and pressure you apply to the comb and create slightly irregular lines. Before you begin the next pass, wipe excess glaze from the comb with a slightly damp cloth or paper towel.

WORK WITH A PARTNER.

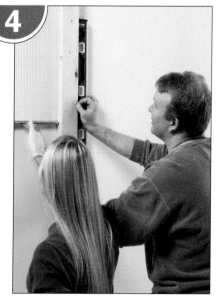

To create very straight and crisp pinstripes, work with a partner. Roll glaze onto the surface in bands only as wide as your combing tool. One person holds a straight 2×4 (cut to the total height of the wall) as plumb as possible. Use painter's tape to temporarily attach a carpenter's level to the 2×4 to ensure perpendicular lines. The second person drags the comb from the ceiling to the floor, using the board as a guide.

CAUTION

If you goof while applying the combing technique or you don't like the result of a particular stroke, roll over the section you're unhappy with immediately with a foam roller loaded with additional glaze. Combed-though glaze dries quickly and, once dry, creates a texture that will need to be sanded before reapplying another finish.

COMBING: MOIRÉ, BASKET WEAVE, AND BURLAP

① BASKET-WEAVE EFFECT.

To create a basket-weave texture, roll on the glaze as described on page 58; then select or create a comb that is the desired width of your woven panels. Beginning in an upper corner, drag the comb vertically down far enough to create a square. Lift and wipe off the comb.

② DRAG PERPENDICULARLY.

Lift comb and reposition perpendicular to vertical marks. Use the last vertical line to guide the placement of the comb. Drag horizontally the length of the square. Drag additional squares, alternating the grain and cleaning the comb after each pass.

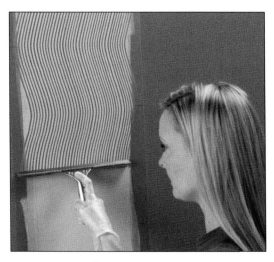

FOR A MOIRÉ EFFECT.

To create a wavy, moiré texture, roll on glaze as described on page 58; then drag the comb tool from the top of the surface to the bottom, pulling the tool at gently varying angles to produce curves. For additional interest, drag atop the first pass of curved lines, alternating the angle of the tool and producing interlacing ripples of glaze and base-coat color.

BURLAP EFFECT

Use a combing tool to mimic the look of burlap fabric. Roll on the glaze as described on page 58; then comb off glaze in consistent horizontal strokes. Use the bottom line of the previous stroke as a guide for the next stroke. While the glaze is still wet, drag the comb vertically through the horizontal stripes to produce a raised, woven texture.

DRAGGING

Dragging, also known as *strié*, is an older, more classic version of the bolder combing techniques (see page 58). Dragging produces delicately interwoven lines, rather than high-contrast stripes of color and glaze. Although dragging looks great as a treatment on an accent wall, you can use this versatile technique for an entire room as well.

YOU'LL NEED

TIME: Half to one day to apply treatment to 400-square-foot area.

SKILLS: Rolling on paint and glaze.

TOOLS: Foam or cloth roller, roller tray, extension rod, weaver brush, stepladder, plumb bob or weighted string, tape measure, color pencil that matches top-coat paint.

MATERIALS: Two closely related shades of latex paint, glaze.

COLOR PENCILS

When you select paint colors for a decorative painting project, consider purchasing color pencils from a crafts or art supply store that match the colors you're planning to work with. (Most crafts and art supply stores now sell a wide array of color pencils individually.) When you make your marks and guidelines in color pencil, you don't need to worry about your lines showing through your paint, as is often the case when you use a regular graphite pencil.

DRAG THROUGH GLAZE.
Dragging a brush through a glaze top coat produces a delicately textured finish that contrasts well with cottage- and garden-style rooms.

1 MARK GUIDELINES.

Apply base-coat paint to the surface and let dry. Use a plumb bob or string weighted down with a washer to mark vertical guidelines every 2 feet or so. Have a partner hold the plumb bob in place (or adhere it to the wall with painter's tape) as you mark lightly along the string with a color pencil that matches the top-coat color.

2 ROLL ON THE GLAZE.

In a plastic container, mix one part glaze, one part paint, and one part water; stir until blended. Pour the glaze mixture into a roller tray. Load a roller with glaze and blot off excess on the tray; then roll the glaze onto the wall. Start at an upper corner and roll down, applying glaze in vertical strokes; use an extension rod to ensure continuous strokes. Apply glaze in a band approximately two roller widths wide.

3 DRAG THE BRUSH THROUGH THE GLAZE.

Standing on top of a stool or small stepladder, press a weaver brush or 8- to 12-inch-wide chip brush against the still-wet glaze, starting at the top edge of the surface. Drag the brush straight down with consistent pressure. As you move down the wall, bend, squat, or slowly step off the stool to keep the motion consistent.

4 CLEAN THE BRUSH.

After each dragging pass, wipe off the glaze-saturated brush with a clean, slightly moist terry-cloth rag. Wipe in the direction of the brush's bristles.

5 DRAG THE SECOND STROKE.

Return to the top of the stool or stepladder. Line up the brush to the right of the finished stroke, overlapping slightly with the edge of the brush. Drag the brush straight down using the same motion to produce a seamless, consistent effect. Wipe off the brush, roll on another band of glaze, and continue the dragging technique farther along the surface. Start adjoining bands quickly so you always will have a wet edge to help blend the bands together.

LINEN

This decorative painting technique has experienced a resurgence in popularity—similar to renewed interest in covering walls with luxurious fabrics such as linen and silk. Like dragging, a softer, more subtle version of pinstripe combing, the linen technique is a more delicate take on the burlap combing technique (see page 59).

Although there are several methods and special products you can use to achieve a linen look, the following technique requires no expensive specialty tools or paints. The technique described here also produces ¼- to ½-inch "seams," which further enhance the illusion of real fabric applied to the walls.

YOU'LL NEED

TIME: One day to apply treatment to a 400-square-foot area.

SKILLS: Rolling on glaze, brushing though glaze, blending brush strokes.

TOOLS: Foam or cloth roller, roller tray, extension rod, weaver brush, painter's tape, tape measure, color pencil, carpenter's level.

MATERIALS: Two closely related shades of latex paint, glaze.

WEAVE SOFT TEXTURE.

By replicating the fabric's texture and the appearance of seams, the linen decorative paint technique is an excellent fool-the-eye choice when you desire the look of luxurious fabric without spending extra money.

1 PREPARE THE SURFACE.

Paint the surface with the base color and let dry. At the ceiling line, use the tape measure to mark increments of 18 or 24 inches. Choose one side of the pencil marks to apply painter's tape, starting at the ceiling and running to the bottom. Apply the tape in plumb, straight strips with the help of a carpenter's level. Burnish the tape with a plastic knife or your fingernail to ensure a tight fit to the wall. Apply tape on all surfaces where the linen technique will be applied.

2 ROLL ON THE GLAZE.

In a plastic container, mix one part glaze, one part paint, and one part water; stir until blended. Pour the glaze mixture into a roller tray. Load the roller with glaze, blot off the excess on the tray; then roll the glaze onto the wall between every other pair of taped lines. Roll on the glaze with long, floor-to-ceiling strokes.

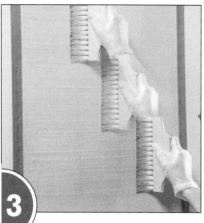

3 DRAG HORIZONTALLY.

Starting at the ceiling line, use a weaver brush, wallpaper brush, or an 8- to 12-inch-wide chip brush to drag level horizontal lines. Work down the wall, overlapping brush strokes ¼ to ½ inch, until you reach the floor.

4 CLEAN THE BRUSH.

After dragging two or three horizontal strokes, wipe off excess glaze using a clean rag or paper towel.

5 DRAG VERTICALLY.

While the glaze is still wet, use a clean brush to drag long, vertical lines from ceiling to floor. Use a steady motion and consistent pressure. Overlap vertical strokes ¼ to ½ inch, dragging horizontal lines across the entire width of a taped-off area.

COLORS FOR CLOTH

To achieve the look of actual linen cloth, select paint colors that mimic the highlights and shadows of fabric. Try the following combinations:

Base coat	Top coat
Golden tan	Yellow
Khaki	Sage green
Gold	Cream
Garnet red	Berry red

Linen *(continued)*

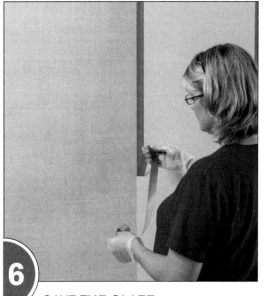

6 SAVE THE GLAZE.

Carefully remove tape and allow glaze-applied sections to dry. While the surface is drying, cover the glaze mixture in the roller tray and mixing container with a damp rag. Wrap rollers and brushes in damp rags as well.

7 PREPARE THE NEXT SECTION.

After the glazed sections are dry, tape off the unpainted sections, using the techniques described on page 63. Position the tape about ½ inch inside the previously painted sections.

DOUBLE UP FOR SPEED

To apply the linen treatment more quickly or to an entire room, work with a partner. Have one person roll on the glaze/paint mixture and the other brush on the linen crosshatching effect. For a consistent look, each person should have the same responsibilities throughout the entire project.

8 ROLL, DRAG, AND DRY.

Roll on glaze top coat with long, vertical strokes and then drag horizontal and vertical lines with the brush. Roll on glaze over the previously painted portion of each section to create a heavier glazed strip that resembles a fabric seam. Remove tape and allow the glaze to dry.

DENIM

For a classic, casual style, denim is a perfect choice. The decorative painting technique inspired by this all-American fabric is equally versatile. Pair two shades of blue paint to get the look of your favorite pair of blue jeans—or try nontraditional color combinations, such as blue and orange or yellow and red, to produce more dynamic results.

APPLY IN STRIPS OR SQUARES

The denim technique works best on wall surfaces when applied in 18- to 24-inch-wide strips or in squares as shown here. Allow ¼- to ½-inch overlap of painted sections to create the appearance of seams. The technique also works well on furniture or cabinetry (with the seam effect), giving the pieces a worn appearance.

YOU'LL NEED

TIME: One day to apply treatment to a 400-square-foot area.

SKILLS: Rolling on glaze, working with a wire loop roller or check roller, taping off sections.

TOOLS: Wire loop roller or check roller, foam or cloth roller, roller tray, screwdriver or paint key, color pencil, painter's tape, tape measure, rags or kraft paper.

MATERIALS: Light blue latex paint for base coat, darker blue latex paint for top coat, glaze.

BRUSH ON CASUAL TEXTURE.

The denim painting technique, applied here in 24×24-inch squares, gives a room a comfortable, casual attitude that blends well with country- and cottage-style decorating. It's great in a child's room too.

Denim *(continued)*

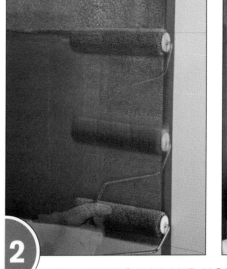

1 MARK THE GRID.

Apply base-coat paint to the surface and let dry. Use a tape measure to mark off a grid of 24×24-inch squares. Tape off every other section with painter's tape. (Refer to pages 62 and 120 for more on taped designs.) In a plastic container, mix one part glaze and three parts paint; stir until blended. Pour the glaze mixture into a roller tray. Load a foam roller with glaze; then roll glaze onto taped-off areas.

2 ROLL VERTICALLY AND HORIZONTALLY.

Roll a wire loop roller or check roller over the wet glaze to create the grain of denim fabric. Roll in one direction (horizontal or vertical), using a straight and consistent motion in each taped-off section. The direction of the motion affects the appearance of the fabric's graining. For additional contrast, plan to roll different taped-off sections in different, perpendicular directions. When the roller no longer removes glaze, clean off the roller by rolling it over kraft paper or wiping it with a lint-free rag.

3 WORK IN TIGHT SPACES.

In corners and other tight spots, use a metal key, flathead screwdriver, or paint opener to mimic the patterning created by the wire loop roller or check roller. Feather in your hand-done crosshatches with those created by the roller. Wipe your tool frequently on a clean rag. Remove tape around painted sections, allow glaze to dry, and then tape the adjoining section, allowing for ¼- to ½-inch overlap of painted areas.

CONVINCING FAUX FABRICS

To enhance the illusion of actual fabric, pay attention to the size and placement of the panels you tape off. Most fabric is sold in standard widths, between 36 and 48 inches. As you plan your decorative painting project, visit a fabric store and find out the typical width for the fabric you're attempting to mimic in paint. Carefully measure the room so you can plan out how you'll tape off the panels. Try to center as many full-width panels as possible on each wall, placing partial-width panels at the corners. Use color pencils that match your top-coat paint to minimize erasing time after the treatment is complete.

PLASTER FRESCO

Although plaster fresco dates to the time of ancient Greece and Rome, the technique described here takes some decidedly modern shortcuts. Rather than applying dozens of layers of tinted clay to a wall, you accomplish this technique simply by troweling one layer of fast-drying drywall compound—available premixed or as a powder at home centers and hardware stores—over primed walls. Two layers of glaze finish the effect.

YOU'LL NEED

TIME: One day to apply treatment to a 400-square-foot area.

SKILLS: Mixing drywall compound, glazing textured surfaces.

TOOLS: Drywall trough, plaster trowel or 10- to 12-inch putty knife, sanding block, fine sandpaper, dust mask, 3-inch brush, paint pads, soft rags, 4- or 5-inch blending brush.

MATERIALS: Drywall compound, medium-color latex paint, white latex paint, glaze.

CAUTION

TRY A LITTLE FIRST.

Although attractive, plaster fresco produces a textured surface that requires extensive sanding to return the surface to its original condition. Before applying plaster fresco to an entire room, try the technique on an accent wall or architectural feature to make sure you like it.

APPLY RAISED TEXTURE.

Give brand-new walls instant character by applying the plaster fresco technique and a glaze wash. The texture of this treatment depends on what tool you use to apply plaster to the wall. A long-nap roller, stiff brush, putty knife, or plaster trowel each produces different effects.

ANCIENT-LOOKING COLORS WORK BEST

Plaster fresco looks best with colors that actually appear on ancient frescos. For your project, select multiple tones of gold, yellow, warm gray, or peach to replicate the look of the clay and plaster found in various regions of the world.

Plaster fresco *(continued)*

1 SPREAD DRYWALL COMPOUND.

Fill a drywall trough with wet drywall compound. If using drywall compound powder, mix the compound following the manufacturer's directions. Load a large plaster trowel or 12-inch putty knife and apply the compound to the wall in strokes thick enough to show the edges of the blade. Start in an upper corner and work down and out.

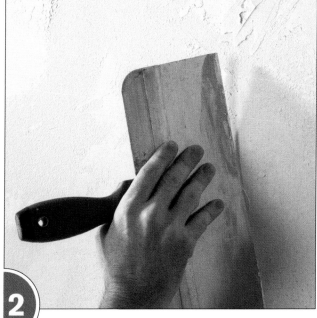

2 ENHANCE THE TEXTURE.

With each stroke of the trowel or blade, lift the tool up at the end of the movement to create a raised, stuccolike surface. Before the plaster begins to dry, return to areas that appear light on plaster or lack adequate texture. Apply small additional amounts of plaster to these areas.

3 SAND THE FINISH.

After the compound has dried (follow manufacturer's recommendations), sand off high spots and rough patches with fine sandpaper. Wear a dust mask while sanding. Brush off the wall or run a vacuum cleaner brush attachment over the surface to remove dust.

CAUTION

THIN LAYERS ARE BEST

Applying a thin layer of drywall compound is crucial to achieving good results with this technique. Thickly applied compound tends to crack and crumble. If you want to add more drywall compound, allow the first layer to completely dry, and then apply another thin layer.

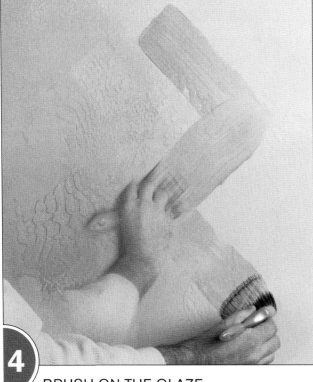

4 BRUSH ON THE GLAZE.

In a plastic mixing container, combine one part glaze with two parts color latex paint; stir well. Use a 3-inch brush to paint the mixture onto the plastered surface. Apply the glaze using a random, small crosshatching movement. Drywall compound soaks up paint, so reload the brush frequently. Work glaze into all cracks and crevices.

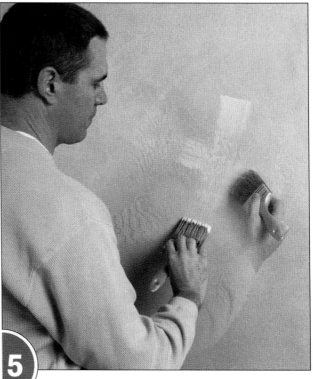

5 RUB ON THE ACCENT GLAZE.

In another plastic mixing container, combine one part glaze, two parts color latex paint, and one part white latex paint; adjust the amount of color and white to create the desired lighter shade. Use a paint pad, brush, or rag to dab the lighter glaze atop the still-wet darker glaze. Apply lighter glaze using a similar crosshatching movement. Leave some areas uncovered by the lighter glaze.

6 BLEND THE GLAZES.

Before the glazes dry, blend the two colors with a clean paint pad (shown) or a soft 4- or 5-inch blending brush. Allow glaze to collect in cracks and crevices for an aged effect. Work the glaze to create highlights (areas with less glaze) and shadows (areas with heavier glaze). Clean the brush or pad frequently with slightly soapy water; then blot tool dry, and continue working the glaze.

AGING

Over time, the colors in paint, fabric, stained wood, and wallpaper tend to fade and take on a richer patina. Sunlight, grease from cooking, and dust from heating sources all contribute to the aging effect, giving colors a yellow, golden, brown, or gray cast.

The aging technique featured here enables you to give new wallpapered or painted surfaces an antique appearance in just a few hours. The amount and color of paint you mix with glaze affect whether a surface appears lightly sun-faded, darkly smoke-stained, or any number of the shades and intensities in between.

YOU'LL NEED

TIME: One day to apply treatment to a 400-square-foot area.

SKILLS: Mixing glazes.

TOOLS: Foam roller, roller tray, sea sponge or rag, bucket of clean water, toothbrush or small chip brush, mixing containers.

MATERIALS: Brown, black, and gold artist's paints, glaze.

ADD AGE WITH ARTIST'S COLORS

Rely on acrylic artist's paints from a crafts or art supply store to tint your aging glaze. Begin tinting your aging glaze with raw umber or burnt sienna, whichever color of brown looks better with your wallpaper or painted base coat. Add small amounts of black or deep gold artist's paints, as desired.

ENHANCE WITH AGE.

Various decorative painting techniques—such as rolling on an aging glaze and flicking on dark brown paint spots to resemble flyspecks—give this room a romantic Victorian feel.

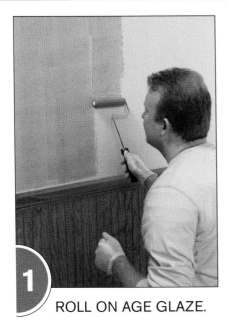

1 ROLL ON AGE GLAZE.

Paint or apply wallpaper to the surface; let dry. In a plastic container, thoroughly mix glaze and burnt sienna or raw umber artist's paint. Apply tinted glaze to a sample board covered with paint or wallpaper that matches walls. Add more brown—or gold or black—artist's paint to achieve the desired tint. Pour mixed glaze into a roller tray and use a foam roller to apply glaze to the surface. Roll on glaze in an overlapping "W" pattern in 4-foot-square sections.

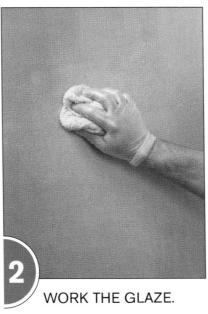

2 WORK THE GLAZE.

Wearing rubber gloves, use a sea sponge or a clean, soft rag to remove and thin portions of the still-wet glaze. Dab the sponge or rag lightly against the surface. Rotate your wrist, reposition your arm, and dab again to create a softly mottled surface.

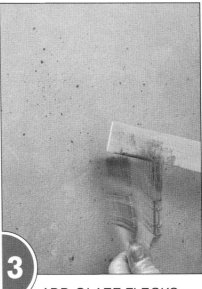

3 ADD GLAZE FLECKS.

In a small plastic container, mix one part brown artist's paint and one part glaze. After the aging glaze dries, load a toothbrush or small chip brush with brown glaze and spatter paint on the wall to look like flyspecks, using your wrist and a plastic knife in a quick, flicking motion. If desired, you can mix a second, lighter brown glaze mixture and apply more flyspecks.

SUN-FADED VS. TEA-STAINED VS. SMOKE-STAINED

The amount of acrylic artist paint you mix with glaze determines the intensity of aging glaze. Here, aging glaze in three intensities has been applied to the same floral wallpaper. Although no set recipes exist for these levels of aging, the looks are best described as (left to right) sun-faded, tea-stained, and smoke-stained.

Whitewashing has been around for centuries. The semitransparent mixture of paint and water produces a finish that's clean and fresh without feeling too crisp and sterile. A great complement to cottage, coastal, and country decors, whitewashing can be applied to just about any surface with a wood grain: paneling, trim, doors, floors, and more.

YOU'LL NEED

TIME: One day to apply treatment to a 400-square-foot area.

SKILLS: Mixing whitewash, distressing wood surfaces, applying whitewash.

TOOLS: Sandpaper, sandpaper block, dust mask, tack cloth, 3- or 4-inch brush, mixing containers.

MATERIALS: White latex paint, water, polyurethane.

APPLY A TRANSPARENT WASH.

Pair whitewashed walls or furniture with light, bright colors for contrast. Pretty floral, print, and striped fabrics work well with the muted softness of this technique.

WHITEWASHING BRINGS OUT DETAILS

Although you can whitewash almost any wood item, whitewashing really shines on projects that feature carved details, turned legs, and interesting grains. Wood furniture can be new and unstained, or a painted flea market find. Whatever the condition of the piece you're working on, thoroughly sand or strip the surface. Whitewash can be applied over stained wood, but you also may be able to remove the stain color with wood bleach before whitewashing.

1 PREPARE THE SURFACE.

Lightly sand the entire surface to be whitewashed with fine-grit sandpaper and a sanding block. Wear a dust mask. Depending on the condition of the surface you're working with, you may need to use a heavier-grit sandpaper first. Some heavily painted surfaces may require chemical stripping. Clean the surface with a tack cloth to remove any dust or paint particles.

2 BRUSH ON WHITEWASH.

In a plastic container, mix two parts white latex paint and one part water. Brush on this whitewash with a 3-inch brush, making long strokes and following the wood grain. Work quickly and in small sections, because whitewash dries in a few minutes.

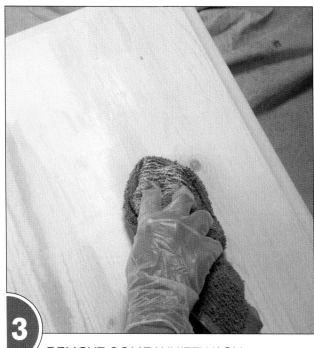

3 REMOVE SOME WHITEWASH.

While the whitewash is still wet, wipe down the surface with a clean, lint-free rag to remove some of the finish and reveal more wood grain. When your rag no longer absorbs whitewash, switch to a new rag. Allow whitewash to dry. If desired, apply another coat of whitewash.

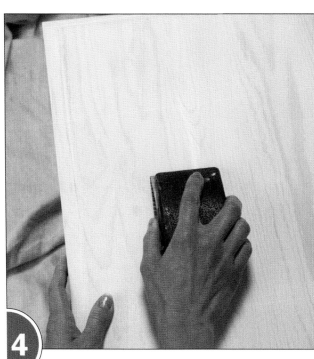

4 DISTRESS THE SURFACE.

After whitewash dries, lightly sand the surface and reveal more of the wood grain on flat surfaces as well as unpainted wood around raised details.

CAUTION

SEAL THE SURFACE

Whitewashed surfaces need to be sealed after the technique is applied and sanded to make the surface easier to keep clean. Brush on two coats of clear, satin polyurethane (or slightly tinted polyurethane, if you prefer) with long, consistent brush strokes. Let dry. Rub lightly with a fine nylon abrasive pad between coats.

DISTRESSING

istressing describes a host of techniques and tricks that decorative painters use to transform new or everyday wood furniture and surfaces into pieces with vintage charm and character. The main technique described here involves applying two layers of contrasting paint and then sanding the surface to reveal underlayers of paint and bare wood.

For the appearance of additional use, you can further distress any surface by hitting it with a hammer, meat cleaver, screwdriver, or a ring of keys.

YOU'LL NEED

TIME: Two days to apply treatment to 100 square feet of cabinetry.

SKILLS: Preparing wood surfaces, painting with a brush, distressing by hand.

TOOLS: Sandpaper, tack cloth, dust mask.

MATERIALS: Light-color latex paint for base coat, darker-color latex paint for top coat, tinted polyurethane.

LOOK AT THE REAL THING

Examine real antiques to learn where furniture gets worn and damaged first. Generally, paint and stain rub off along edges and on trim and raised features. Flat panels and inset surfaces receive less wear and tear. For a natural-looking finished product, let your research affect how and where you distress your projects.

AGE NEW SURFACES.

Distressing wood furniture—such as these painted, sanded, and stained cabinets—is a time-consuming, labor-intensive process. But the one-of-kind finish that results can be well worth the effort.

1 PREPARE THE SURFACE.

Lightly sand the entire surface to be distressed. Use fine-grit sandpaper (or medium-grit, followed by fine-grit) to prepare the wood. Wear a dust mask. Depending on the desired results, you generally don't need to completely remove all stain or paint from the wood. Simply remove the shine from the wood and get it ready to absorb fresh paint. Wipe the sanded surface with a tack cloth.

2 BRUSH ON THE FIRST COLOR.

Using a 3-inch trim brush, apply the undercoat of latex paint. Paint with the grain of the wood. Let dry. Based on your decorating needs, the undercoat can be lighter or darker than the top-coat color; the contrast between the colors of the layers is more important.

3 BRUSH ON THE SECOND COLOR.

Using a new or clean 3-inch trim brush, apply the top-coat color of latex paint. Brush with the grain. Let dry. For an old, often-painted look, build up extra paint on inside corners and in the bottoms of details.

4 SAND AND SCRAPE.

Using fine-grit sandpaper, sand the edges, raised portions, and details of the surface, revealing the undercoat and spots of bare wood. Sand a few flat areas of the surface as well, attempting to replicate where actual use and wear might occur. Wipe with a tack cloth. For a more well-used look, you can hit the surface with metal tools, keys, or other objects.

5 TINT AND PROTECT.

With a new brush, apply a coat of tinted, clear polyurethane, which gives the surface an aged look. Buy slightly brown- or gray-tinted polyurethane at a paint store or home center, or mix your own by adding brown or black artist's acrylic paint to clear, acrylic-based polyurethane. Let dry. Buff the finish with a fine nylon pad. Apply a second coat.

CRACKLE

Genuine crackled paint can be the result of extreme changes of temperature, sun and rain damage, an inappropriately prepared surface, or poor-quality paint. And yet, crackled finishes—real or created through decorative paint techniques—have a charm and uniqueness that few other surface treatments can rival.

The secret to creating crackle finishes today is the application of a colorless crackle medium before applying a coat of latex paint. Crackle medium is available at home centers and paint stores. Due to the wide range of resulting crackle finishes, experiment with your application technique and color choices on sample boards (see page 41) before applying to a surface.

CRACKLE TEXTURE.

The crackle-finish top coat on this new wood table almost seems to pop with energy. Although white or cream undercoats are most typical of a crackle finish, you can pair your top-coat color with any contrasting color for the undercoat.

(see page 41)

YOU'LL NEED

TIME: One day to apply treatment.

SKILLS: Applying crackle medium, rolling on paint.

TOOLS: Foam or cloth roller, roller tray, paintbrush, old towels, stippling brush or thick, stiff chip brush.

MATERIALS: Latex paint for base coat and top coat, crackle medium.

MORE WATER FOR FINER CRACKS

The amount of water you mix with the crackle medium also affects the look of the final cracks. Adding more water generally results in fewer and finer cracks. Experiment with adding water to crackle medium on sample boards before applying to a surface.

1 PREPARE THE SURFACE.

Lightly sand the entire surface. Use fine-grit sandpaper (or medium-grit, followed by fine-grit) to prepare the wood to receive paint. Wear a dust mask. You do not need to remove all stain or paint; simply remove the shine from the wood. Wipe the sanded surface with a tack cloth. For a smooth undercoat, use a roller or brushes to apply the base-coat paint. Let dry.

② APPLY CRACKLE MEDIUM.

Apply the crackle medium with a brush, roller, or rag. The tool you use and the direction in which you apply crackle medium both affect the final crackle result. In many cases, the medium works best if applied in both directions—check the instructions for the product you are using. See the tip box below for tool and application options.

BRUSH IT ON OR ROLL IT ON

You can apply crackle medium with a brush or a roller. Brushed-on crackle medium results in cracks that follow the general direction of the brush stroke. Heavily rolled crackle medium produces tiny, hairline cracks. Lightly rolled medium results in wider, thicker cracks.

CAUTION

FOLLOW THE LABEL

For best results, always follow the manufacturer's instructions for the specific brand of crackle medium you're using. Crackle mediums vary in the amount of set time required, the amount of time you have before the medium is no longer usable, and the number of coats of medium to apply.

③ APPLY TOP-COAT PAINT.

Following manufacturer's instructions, allow the crackle medium to set and then apply the top-coat paint with a brush or roller. Apply paint in one direction, with the grain of the wood. The top coat begins crackling in a few seconds. Let dry. For furniture or high-traffic surfaces, apply one or two coats of clear, satin polyurethane to protect the finish.

CRACKLE VARIATIONS

You can pair any two colors for the base coat and undercoat used in crackle finish. Additionally, the way you apply the crackle medium affects the crackling pattern.

Here, a dark base-coat color is paired with a light top coat. The crackle medium was applied with both vertical and horizontal brush strokes, resulting in a smaller and more irregular crackle pattern.

Here, a light base-coat color is paired with a dark top coat. The crackle medium was applied with long, continuous brush strokes in one direction, producing longer, more dramatic crackles.

FAUX LEATHER

Faux leather is one of the most popular decorative paint finishes. Do-it-yourselfers and professional decorative painters have dozens of methods for creating faux leather finishes. The technique described here combines the tools, techniques, and materials that produce good, consistent results. While faux leather is a challenging decorative painting technique, you can achieve beautiful results with practice and careful application.

The method described here is labor-intensive, but you can find specialty faux-leather paints and all-in-one kits at home centers and paint stores. Most of these products produce attractive results, but often at a premium price.

CREATE A HANDSOME TEXTURE.

The faux leather treatment applied to the lower portion of a wainscoted wall gives this den a refined air. Select colors for a faux leather treatment based on the most common colors of real leather—chocolate brown, deep burgundy, rich camel, and deep plum.

YOU'LL NEED

TIME: One day to apply treatment to a 400-square-foot area.

SKILLS: Combining colors, rolling on glazes, manipulating glazes.

TOOLS: Foam roller, roller tray, chamois cloth, bucket of clean water, towels.

MATERIALS: Medium-color latex paint for base coat, darker-color latex paint for top coat, glaze.

START SMALL BEFORE PAINTING A WALL

After practicing the faux leather technique on a few sample boards, try the technique on a smaller project—such as a wooden storage box or the top of an end table—before attempting an entire wall or other large surface.

1 ROLL ON PATCHES OF GLAZE.

Apply base-coat paint to the surface and let dry. In a plastic container, mix one part glaze, one part paint, and one part water; stir until blended. Pour the glaze into a roller tray. Load the roller with glaze and roll off the excess on the tray. Roll on a 2-foot-square section of darker glaze in irregular patches, reproducing the appearance and shape of a swatch of leather.

2 BLEND THE GLAZES.

Moisten and wring a chamois cloth. Holding the cloth in a flat-sided pom-pom, pat along the edge of the irregular shape, softening and blending the edges as you push the glaze out and around the shape. Rotate your wrist and adjust the placement of your hand as you work your way around the edge.

3 SOFTEN THE GLAZES.

Adjust the pom-pom of cloth to work with a clean portion and pounce on the center of the shape, removing glaze to create areas of highlights and shadows. Rotate your wrist and reposition your hand frequently.

MORE WAYS TO GET THE LOOK OF LEATHER

Tweak the paints and tools you use to produce a range of leather textures and grains. Get familiar with the various types of leather grains by examining leather books, handbags, upholstered furniture, and clothing. Try incorporating any of the following ideas to further simulate the look of leather:

Use frottage. Use the frottage technique described on pages 52–53 as the basis for your leather-look treatment. Rather than applying squares of plastic or cotton sheeting, cut out irregular pieces of sheeting and press them into a top coat of wet glaze. Look at leather scraps at a fabric or upholstery store to get an idea of common shapes.

Use a stipple brush. Roll on an irregularly shaped patch of top-coat glaze, as outlined on page 78, and then pounce on the glaze with a stipple brush or stiff hand brush. Use a tightly swirling or rubbing motion, lifting the brush at the end of each stroke. The resulting dappled texture resembles leather that's been more roughly tanned or sueded.

Use a two-step kit. Look for specialty paint kits that combine a clear or tinted sizing product and a tinted top-coat glaze. Following the manufacturer's instructions, brush on the sizing in patches, using overlapping brushstrokes. Apply the top coat and allow the glaze to pool and settle into a richly grained leather texture.

Faux leather *(continued)*

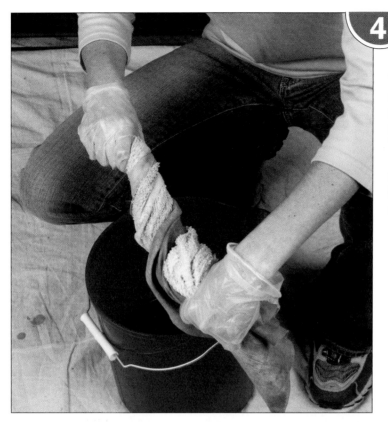

4

CLEAN AND DRY THE CHAMOIS CLOTH.

When your chamois cloth no longer has any unglazed portions, or when it appears you're applying glaze rather than absorbing it, rinse out the chamois cloth in a bucket of clean water. Wring several times to remove glaze.

Wring excess water from the rinsed chamois cloth. If necessary, roll the chamois cloth tightly in an old, dry terry-cloth towel to remove even more water.

SUBSTITUTES FOR CHAMOIS

While chamois cloth is the best choice for this technique, it is also expensive. You can substitute smooth, fine-grained, natural-fiber cheesecloth. Launder and dry the cheesecloth to increase its softness and remove lint and loose fibers. Avoid polyester and roughly woven cheesecloth; they yield a finish that more closely resembles fabric than tanned leather.

5

STIPPLE THE ACCENT TEXTURE.

Dip a stippling brush or a thick chip brush into the roller tray and blot off excess. On the surface you're painting, tap additional highlights and shadows onto the nearly dry top coat. Mark off smaller, irregular sections within the 2-foot-square area you're working, replicating the detailed graining of actual leather.

6 ROLL ON NEXT AREA.

Load the foam roller with more glaze and roll on another irregular patch of glaze next to the finished section. Allow an unglazed gap of about ¼ inch between the sections.

7 WORK GLAZE.

Using a ball of clean or new chamois, pounce along the edges between the new and older sections to create a seamlike effect between sections. Don't worry about completely blending the edges. Continue working the glaze and rolling on additional sections of glaze as previously described.

CAUTION

CLEAN THE CHAMOIS WHEN IT WON'T LIFT GLAZE

When applying the faux leather technique, you know it's time to rinse or replace your chamois cloth when it no longer pulls glaze off the wall.

SUEDE

The soft, matte texture of suede inspires one of the most sought-after decorative painting finishes. While you can purchase specialty suede tools and paints that have small plastic or resin beads added to the traditional paint ingredients, the following technique relies on basic tools, paints, and glazes. Careful, consistent application of paint and glaze will ensure success.

A key to creating a convincing suede finish is to limit the amount of glaze you mix with paint and water. Less water makes the top coat less transparent, which gives you a look that more closely resembles the brushed nap of suede.

YOU'LL NEED

TIME: One day to apply treatment to a 400-square-foot area.

SKILLS: Mixing glazes, applying glaze to surface, working glaze with rags.

TOOLS: Foam or cloth roller, roller tray, mixing container, 3-inch brush or chip brush, knit rags, cheesecloth.

MATERIALS: Light golden-tan latex paint for base coat, medium golden-tan latex paint for top coat, glaze.

CAUTION

CONSISTENCY COUNTS

Successful application of the suede treatment requires consistent application of glaze. For this reason, only one person should apply the top coat for the entire surface you're covering.

SOFTEN WITH SUEDE.

Soft suede walls in buttery tan are a perfect addition to a study or bedroom. Use knit rags and cheesecloth to mimic the rugged, yet soft finish of actual suede.

SUEDE IN A FLASH

For a fast suede finish, look for prepackaged suede kits and aerosol cans of specially formulated suede paint. While more expensive, these kits enable you to produce the look of suede on smaller surfaces and accent pieces in minutes.

1 APPLY TOP-COAT GLAZE.

Apply base-coat paint to the surface and let dry. In a plastic container, mix one part glaze, two parts paint, and one part water; stir until blended. Pour the glaze into a roller tray. Brush on glaze with a 3-inch brush. Apply the glaze in a series of long, overlapping lines, with squiggly edges, over an area about 2 feet square.

2 POUNCE ON THE GLAZE.

Moisten and wring out several soft knit rags. Holding a rag in a loose pom-pom (see page 49), spread out the glaze using a small, circular motion, similar to scrubbing a pot. Soften the edges of the applied glaze while still allowing some of the irregular lines and shapes to remain.

3 TAP FOR TEXTURE.

Tap the near-dry glaze with a pom-pom of coarse, moistened cheesecloth, using the same small, rotating movement. Create highlights and shadows within the glazed inner portions of the lines. Rearrange the cheesecloth pom-pom in your hand frequently so you're always using clean cloth.

Suede *(continued)*

4 CLEAN AS YOU GO.

When the knit rags and cheesecloth are saturated with glaze and no longer remove glaze from the wall, wash them out in a bucket of clean water. Wring out rags for later use.

5 APPLY NEXT GLAZE AREA.

Moving to the side of the completed section, brush on another series of overlapping, squiggly lines. Allow the new section to touch only the lightest portions of the completed section.

6 WORK THE GLAZE.

Using clean, moist rags, manipulate the glaze with a small, circular motion, similar to the motion of scrubbing a pot. Feather the fresh glaze into the previously completed section. Avoid overblending. Keep the texture in the new section consistent with, but not necessarily identical to, the texture in the previous section.

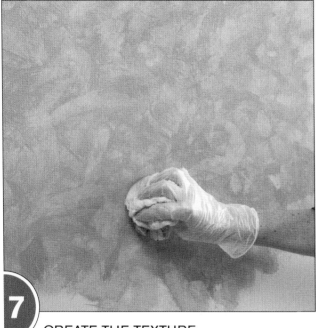

7 CREATE THE TEXTURE.

Tap the second, nearly dry section of glaze with a pom-pom of coarse, moistened cheesecloth. Create highlights and shadows within the glazed inner portions of the lines.

WORKING WITH SPECIALTY SUEDE PAINT AND TOOLS

You also can create the look of suede walls by using specialty paints and tools available at most home centers and paint stores. These products are available from a variety of manufacturers, but in general, they work like this:

■ Use a small sponge roller to roll on suede paint around edges of the surface.

■ Use a larger specialty sponge roller to roll on paint in a consistent vertical direction to the majority of the surface.

■ While rolled-on paint is still wet, use a 3-inch brush to apply additional suede paint using a small crisscrossing or cross-hatching movement.

Suede paint can be difficult to touch up after it has dried. For any surface or portion of a surface where you choose to add a second coat, apply the suede paint using numerous cross-hatching brushstrokes to blend in your work. Maintain a wet edge if you apply an entire second coat of suede paint.

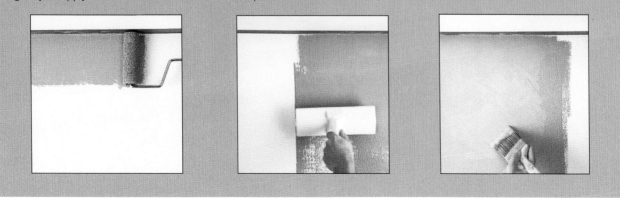

GRANITE

As a surface choice, natural granite is durable, timeless, and—unfortunately—expensive. This decorative painting treatment is a cost-effective solution if you love the look of granite but can't afford its price tag.

The granite decorative paint treatment is most effective in smaller doses and when applied to surfaces and structures that could be made of actual granite. Apply this treatment to tabletops, countertops, accessories, mantels, or architectural trimwork to get the best results.

YOU'LL NEED

TIME: One day to apply treatment to a 200-square-foot area.

SKILLS: Preparing wood surfaces for painting, selecting appropriate paint colors, sponging on glaze, applying polyurethane finish.

TOOLS: Fine-grit sandpaper, sandpaper block, tack cloth, straightedge, tape measure, carpenter's square, 3- to 5-inch brush, paint sticks, sea sponge, mixing containers, four paint trays or plates, painter's tape, artist's brush, steel wool.

MATERIALS: Four colors of latex paint (one color to serve as base coat), glaze, black artist's paint, gloss polyurethane.

TRANSFORM SURFACES.

Make a flea market find look like a treasured family heirloom by painting a faux granite insert panel. Here, light orange, light tan, rust, and brown glazes are applied atop a medium orange base coat to create the illusion of real stone.

1 PREPARE THE SURFACE.

Lightly sand the entire surface that will receive the granite paint treatment. Depending on the condition of the surface, you may need to use a coarse-grit sandpaper, followed by fine-grit sandpaper. Clean the surface with a tack cloth to remove dust or paint particles.

2 MASK OFF THE AREA.

With painter's tape, mask off the area where the granite paint treatment will be applied. Burnish the edge of the tape tightly to the surface with a fingernail. To create a faux granite tabletop insert as shown here, use a pencil, straightedge, and carpenter's square to mark off the area to be painted.

3 BRUSH ON THE BASE COAT.

Brush on the base-coat paint within the taped-off area. Let dry. Apply a second coat if working with bare wood.

4 SELECT APPROPRIATE COLORS.

In small, separate mixing containers combine one part glaze, two parts paint, and one part water; stir until blended. For help selecting colors see tip boxes below and on page 88. Pour equal amounts of each glaze color into separate shallow plates or trays.

MATCH COLORS TO THE REAL THING

Getting the right combination and application of paint colors is critical for a convincing faux granite finish. Examine various types of real granite at home centers, design centers, and stone product manufacturers. When you find a type of granite that you like for its coloration and texture, ask the sales representative for a sample. (Samples are often free or priced under $5.) Use the sample as guide for paint colors and texture.

Granite *(continued)*

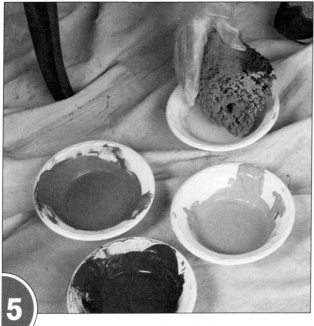

5 APPLY COLORS EQUALLY.

Use a paint stick to dab each of the glaze colors onto a moistened sea sponge. Dab on the glaze in specific, roughly equally sized areas of the sponge. Avoid blending and mixing the glazes.

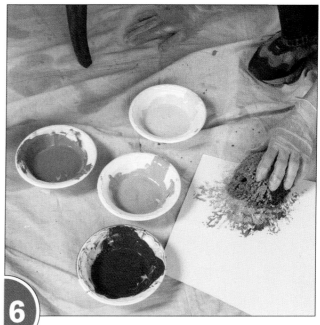

6 EVALUATE THE COLOR BALANCE.

Blot the glaze-laden sponge on a piece of poster board or paper to remove excess glaze. Check the balance of the glaze colors.

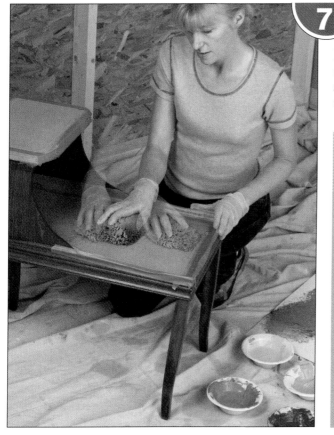

7 DAB ON THE COLORS.

Pat the sponge onto the surface. Avoid pressing too hard and overapplying the glazes. Rotate your wrist and dab the sponge, overlapping the previous dab. Continue applying the glaze in a random, rotating pattern.

COLOR COMBINATIONS TO TRY

Granite occurs naturally in a variety of colors. Try these paint combinations to simulate various granites:

■ Gray granite: Black base coat; light gray, medium gray, and medium-dark gray glazes.

■ Blue granite: Medium blue base coat; light, medium, and dark blue glazes.

■ Rust or orange granite: Medium orange base coat; light orange, light tan, rust, and brown glazes.

■ Green granite: Dark green base coat; light gray, medium gray, tan, dark gray, and medium green glazes.

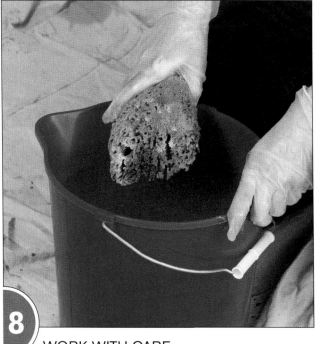

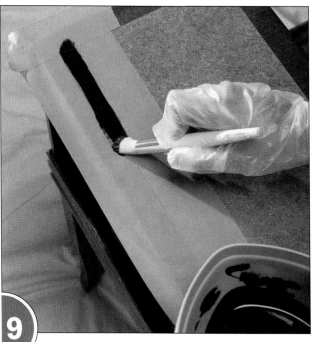

8 WORK WITH CARE.

When the glaze colors become muddied and mixed, rinse out the sponge with clean water. Wring sponge dry. Apply the glazes again with the paint stick, blot the sponge on paper, and continue dabbing on glazes as before. Avoid overworking the glazes; you should be able to see each individual color as part of the treatment. Remove the tape. Let the paint dry.

9 HIGHLIGHT EDGES.

To enhance the appearance of inset granite, apply two strips of painter's tape parallel to each other, about ¼ inch apart around the edge of the painted surface. Burnish the tape tightly to the surface with a fingernail or a plastic burnishing tool. Use an artist's brush to apply black acrylic paint in the space between the two tape strips. Remove tape and let the paint dry.

10 BRUSH ON PROTECTION AND SHINE.

To create the look of polished granite and make the finish more durable, brush on a coat of glossy, clear water-base polyurethane. Let dry. Smooth any ridges with a fine nylon abrasive pad, wipe with a tack cloth, and apply a second coat of polyurethane, if desired.

PROTECT THE EFFECT

Given its high level of detail, the granite decorative paint treatment is not as durable as other decorative paint treatments. Protect the finish—and increase the appearance of actual polished stone—by applying two or three coats of gloss polyurethane.

Painting a surface to look like it is made of stone blocks or bricks is a versatile technique because you can customize the size, shape, arrangement, and color of the blocks or bricks in the finished treatment—much like a master bricklayer designing a custom masonry project. By combining the appropriate paint colors and dimensions, a stone block or brick project can resemble medieval cobblestones, Victorian pavers, modern cinder blocks, or a host of other popular masonry styles.

The thickness of the painter's tape you choose for this technique affects the appearance of the grout lines in your finished project. Look at real masonry projects to get a sense of the mortar thickness that is most appropriate for the type and size of blocks or bricks you want to represent. Look for masking tape in ⅛-, ¼-, ⅜-, and ½-inch thicknesses at art supply and craft or hobby stores.

YOU'LL NEED

TIME: One day to apply treatment to a 400-square-foot area.

SKILLS: Selecting appropriate colors, measuring and marking off walls, applying tape, stippling glaze.

TOOLS: ⅛-, ¼-, ⅜-, or ½-inch tape, carpenter's level, pencil, tape measure, mixing containers, stipple brushes or stiff chip brushes.

MATERIALS: Light gray or taupe latex paint (for base coat and mortar lines), two or three shades of latex paint for top coat, glaze.

IMITATE BRICK PATTERNS.

A wall of stone blocks gives this room the feel of an English conservatory. To avoid overwhelming the eye with strong texture and color, use the brick or block paint technique as wainscoting, on corners, or on an accent wall—similar to the way actual brick would appear on these surfaces.

① MEASURE FOR THE HORIZONTAL JOINTS.

Apply base-coat paint to the wall and let dry. Using a carpenter's level, pencil, and tape measure, mark the placement of the horizontal lines for your design. Start from the bottom of the surface and make small pencil marks; don't draw lines. For the look of stone blocks, as shown here, joints are 8 inches apart.

② TAPE ALONG THE HORIZONTAL JOINTS.

Apply thin painter's or masking tape along the horizontal joint markings. Use a carpenter's level or a partner to help apply level lines. Step back 8 to 10 feet to check your progress often.

③ MARK AND TAPE THE VERTICAL JOINTS.

Hang a plumb bob (or a string with a metal nut tied to one end) from the ceiling to help make the vertical mortar lines plumb. Start from the far left and apply tape, using the plumb bob as a guide. Apply vertical tape strips to every other row of blocks or bricks to create a masonry effect.

④ COMPLETE THE JOINT PATTERN.

Rehang the plumb bob to the right of the first set of vertical lines and tape the next vertical joints, using the string as a guide. For the blocks, vertical joints are 16 inches apart. Standard bricks are approximately 4 inches tall by 8 inches long.

VARY COLORS AND TEXTURES

To create convincing bricks and blocks, you must vary the textures and dominant colors on each taped area. Take a look at real masonry projects to get a sense of the variety of textures and colors present.

CAUTION

The narrow masking tape you will probably use in this technique is stickier than painter's tape and can remove paint from walls when lifted, especially if you leave the masking tape on the surface for a long time. Be sure to apply masking tape to a completely dry surface; allow double or triple the recommended drying time for the base coat. Carefully remove tape as soon as the technique is completed.

WEATHERING YOUR BRICKS

For a weathered effect, let the two glazes used for the bricks dry; then sponge on thinned green glaze (one part paint, two or three parts glaze, one part water) to resemble moss and lichen. For an overall aged effect, remove the tape lines and roll on a very thin coat of gray or brown glaze over the entire treatment.

Blocks and bricks *(continued)*

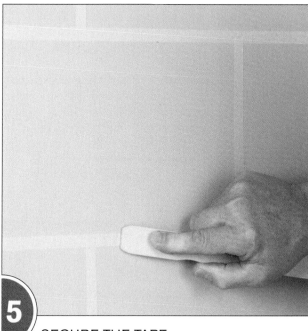

5 SECURE THE TAPE.

Use your fingernail or a burnishing tool to smooth the tape lines to the wall. The tape must adhere tightly to prevent paint from creeping under the edges; that would spoil the effect.

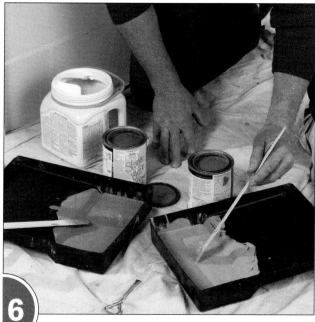

6 LOAD THE BRUSH.

In small, separate mixing containers combine one part glaze and one part paint; stir until blended. Pour equal amounts of each glaze color into separate shallow plates or trays. Load a stipple brush or a stiff chip brush with the glaze that will be the dominant brick color. Blot excess glaze on a piece of newspaper or a rag.

7 TAP ON THE GLAZE.

Working within one taped-off block at a time, tap on the first glaze with the brush. Pounce quickly and randomly, rotating the position of your hand and arm frequently. Apply glaze inconsistently, allowing small patches of the base coat to show through the glaze. Avoid overpouncing and producing an overly blended finish. After completing each block, step back a few feet and evaluate your work; every block should have a distinct look but should still blend with the surrounding blocks.

8 WORK IN THE SECOND GLAZE.

Load a second stipple brush or stiff chip brush with the second glaze color; blot off excess. Working within the same block, apply the second glaze color with the same pouncing motion. Use the second color as an accent, applying glaze to some areas and leaving other areas unglazed. Blend the glazes slightly, but don't overpounce or overblend.

9 MOVE TO THE NEXT BLOCK.

Begin working on another block, applying the first glaze to the entire area of the block and the second glaze as an accent to portions of the block. Allow each block to have slightly different amounts of each glaze and levels of blending for a more realistic look.

10 REMOVE THE TAPE AS YOU WORK.

When you're done painting a section of bricks, carefully remove the masking tape. Start by removing vertical tape pieces, followed by longer, horizontal bands. Regular masking tape left on a surface for days—or even several hours—can pull up paint, plaster, and even drywall when you attempt to remove it. Touch up any areas where top-coat glaze may have seeped under the tape by applying the base-coat paint with an artist's brush.

FAUX MARBLE

For the illusion of grandeur, few finishes can compare to faux marbling. This fool-the-eye paint treatment has been in demand for centuries. As far back as the 1600s, European nobility hired artisans to apply a variety of faux marble finishes to walls, floors, and architectural features in their estates. Even if you can't afford actual marble in your entryway, on countertops, or as a mantelpiece, you still can get the look of real stone with a little practice and attention to detail.

Marbling can be extremely realistic or more stylized. Look at samples of real marble countertops and tile to get a sense of the colors, textures, and tools you need to get a natural-looking result. Or forget about reality and create a custom marble finish using paint colors that work with your decor but may not appear in natural stone.

Professional faux-finishing painters have dozens of tricks and techniques to duplicate marble's intricate texture, intense coloration, and characteristic veining. The technique outlined here provides a foundation for faux marbling, along with a few of the most popular variations.

YOU'LL NEED

TIME: One to two days to cover a 400-square-foot area.

SKILLS: Selecting colors, rolling on paint, ragging on glaze, stippling, detailing with a feather.

TOOLS: Painter's tape, tape measure, carpenter's level, foam or cloth roller, roller tray, soft rags, stippling brush or stiff chip brush, mixing containers, large feather, soft blending brush.

MATERIALS: Medium to dark latex paint for base coat, medium latex paint for top coat, latex paint for veins and details, glaze.

FOOL THE EYE.

A faux marble decorative paint technique applied to this fireplace mantel and surround elevates simple pine to the level of regally crafted stone. Faux marbling usually is most effective in small amounts, where the intricate details and intense color and texture of the technique can grab attention.

FAUX MARBLE DURABILITY

Because faux marbling is a paint treatment, it's much less durable than real marble. Apply marbling to surfaces that receive light wear and use. Avoid applying to frequently used countertops or areas near water sources. If you apply faux marble to a high-traffic area, such as floors or wainscoted walls, brush or roll on at least two coats of clear polyurethane to protect the finished treatment.

1 MASK THE MARBLE AREAS.

Use painter's tape to mask off the edge of any area where you plan to apply faux marbling. Apply faux marbling to surfaces that could actually be carved from marble or covered with marble slabs or tiles. Use a tape measure, carpenter's level, and pencil as appropriate to accurately mark off the area to be painted.

2 APPLY THE BASE COAT.

Pour the base-coat paint into a roller tray or paint bucket, and roll or brush on the base color within the taped-off areas. Let the base coat dry.

3 RUB ON GLAZES.

In a separate mixing container combine one part top-coat paint, two or three parts glaze, and one part water; stir until blended. Pour into a shallow plate or tray. Dampen and wring out a soft rag. Form rag into a soft pom-pom (see page 49) and load with glaze. Blot off excess glaze. Rub glaze onto the surface in a loose, overlapping circular motion. To work with the glaze while it's still wet, work in areas roughly 2 feet square.

Faux marble *(continued)*

4 ENHANCE THE TEXTURE.

Tap the still-wet glaze with a stippling brush or wide, stiff chip brush. Rotate the brush and reposition your arm and hand frequently to create a lightly porous, mottled surface.

5 SOFTEN THE TEXTURE.

Use a soft brush to blend the glaze and eliminate any harsh texture. Avoid overblending, which makes the surface look flat.

CAUTION

Even if you're an experienced decorative painter, practice faux marbling on sample boards (see page 41) prior to applying the treatment to the actual surface. Sample boards give you an opportunity to refine your technique and experiment with combinations of tools, colors, textures, and detailing.

OTHER MARBLE TRICKS AND TOOLS

There are dozens of ways to simulate marble.
Begin with the general technique described here, but add in a few alternative ideas:

Try frottage. Rather than working various colors of glaze, use frottage to create a textured top coat. Brush on one or two colors of top-coat glaze and press on sheets of thin plastic (see pages 52–53 for details). Remove the plastic sheeting and apply veining and other details.

Use a stick. Rather than using a feather to apply details, break off a thin stick or dowel rod and use the jagged end to drag on veins.

Try wet-on-wet. After the base coat dries, brush on a coat of clear, untinted glaze and then, while the glaze is still wet, rub on top-coat paint that's slightly thinned with additional glaze. This wet-on-wet technique makes the glaze and paint mix right on the surface and produces a soft, almost spongy, mottled texture.

6 PAINT ON SOME VEINS.

In a separate container mix veining glaze by combining one part paint and one part glaze. Dip the top two inches of a large feather into the glaze. Starting at the top of the surface, apply veins of paint in a consistent diagonal direction. As you drag the tip of the feather along the surface, twirl the feather between your fingers to create the varying wideness of marble veining. Occasionally, shake the feather as you drag it to create jagged portions.

7 SOFTEN THE VEINS AND SEAL.

Soften any hard edges on the veining with a soft blending brush, following the diagonal direction of the veins. Let the veining dry. Apply one or two coats of matte or satin clear polyurethane for protection and to enhance the illusion of a polished stone surface. Remove tape.

COLOR COMBINATIONS FOR CONVINCING MARBLE

Convincing faux marble treatments require the right choice of colors, as well as refined application techniques. Here are some reliable color combinations to simulate the look of marble. Test any color combination on sample boards before applying it to the actual surface.	Base-coat color	Top-coat color(s)	Veining and detail color
	Ivory	Light gray, medium taupe	Dark taupe
	Light yellow	Medium golden-yellow, medium gray	Dark gray
	Medium orange	Rusty orange, medium brown	White or cream
	Black	Light green, medium green	White
	Peachy-pink	Light peach, Medium gray	White or cream

WOOD GRAINING

Wood graining gives flat, smooth surfaces the warmth and texture of fine wood, without the expense or carpentry skills required to install the real thing. With wood graining, you can transform flat walls into knotty pine paneling, or make a metal desk look like an oak heirloom.

The wood-graining tool, also known as a rocker, is the key to achieving good results with this technique. The graining tool features a ridged rubber pad attached to a curved head. By dragging the tool through wet glaze and rocking the handle, you selectively remove thin strips of glaze and produce the appearance of wavy wood grain. By varying the glaze colors, adjusting the speed at which you rock the tool, and painting in freehand details like knots and cracks, you can create the look of specific kinds of wood.

YOU'LL NEED

TIME: One day to apply treatment to a 400-square-foot area.

SKILLS: Selecting paint colors and mimicking wood tones, rolling on paint and glaze, using wood-graining tool.

TOOLS: Cloth or foam roller, roller tray, mixing container, 3-inch brush, wood-graining tool, soft brush.

MATERIALS: Light latex paint for base coat, medium to dark latex paint for top coat, glaze.

MIX IT UP

You don't have to select glazes that match the hues found in actual wood. You can drag the graining tool through layers of any contrasting glaze to produce an intriguing moiré pattern.

REFINE A PLAIN SURFACE.

Give a metal six-panel door the appearance of richly stained oak by dragging a wood-graining tool through a deep red glaze top coat and revealing a warm pecan base coat beneath it.

1 APPLY GLAZE.

Thoroughly clean and prepare the surface to be painted. Metal, pressboard, and laminate each require special preparation and priming; consult with a home center or paint store employee. Roll or brush on base-coat paint; let dry. In a plastic container, mix three parts glaze and one part paint; stir until blended. The glaze dries quickly, so brush on glaze in 10- to 12-inch-wide sections that match the dimensions of real boards.

2 CREATE THE ILLUSION OF WOOD GRAIN.

Starting at the top or far end of a glazed section, press and drag the wood-graining tool, rocking the handle back and forth in a steady, straight motion.

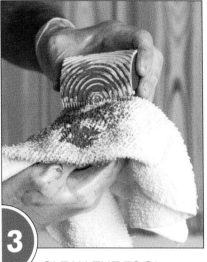

3 CLEAN THE TOOL.

After each dragging pass, wipe excess glaze from the rubber head of the wood-graining tool with a clean, moist cloth or paper towel.

4 DRAG ANOTHER PASS.

For the next strip of graining, press and drag the graining tool through the glaze, slightly overlapping the texture made during the first pass. Rock the graining tool in a steady motion, but vary the placement of knots from those in the first pass.

5 SOFTEN GRAINING.

While the glaze is still wet, brush lightly and perpendicular to the grain with a soft, clean brush to create a worn effect.

6 MOVE TO THE NEXT SECTION.

Brush on glaze to another section of the surface and continue using the graining tool as previously described.

CAUTION

Although you could use wood graining to create the look of a hardwood floor, the treatment is best suited for lower-traffic surfaces. Brush or roll on two coats of clear polyurethane to increase the durability of any wood-grained surface.

PAINTED DOORS

Most new metal doors, such as the one shown on these pages, are sold ready to paint. Wood graining shouldn't be applied to the exterior side of a door; sun and water damage will quickly destroy the treatment.

STENCILED BORDER

Few decorative painting techniques offer more graphic impact than stenciling. Fortunately, the range of stencil options—including paints, applicators, and precut stencil designs—has continued to expand since the heyday of stenciling in the 1980s. Stencil paints are available as powders, liquids, pastes, or solids. Applicators range from inexpensive disposable foam pads to high-quality horsehair brushes.

Decorative painters have dozens of opinions about which materials, products, and tools work best, as well as the best locations to apply a stenciled motif. If you're new to stenciling, try working with inexpensive brushes and liquid stencil paint first. The application technique is similar regardless of the tools or paints you use. Because stenciling supplies can be expensive, build up your kit of tools and paints gradually as you work on specific projects.

ADD COLOR AND ATTITUDE.

A simple stenciled border applied near the ceiling line uses several colors and subtle shading to give the room greater architectural appeal.

YOU'LL NEED

TIME: One day to apply treatment to 40 linear feet.

SKILLS: Selecting stencil motifs, cutting stencils, applying paint to stencils, planning a treatment.

TOOLS: Stencil pads or brushes (one for each color to be applied), painter's tape, rags, carpenter's level, plastic stencil, tape measure, pencil, artist's brush.

MATERIALS: Latex paint for base coat, latex stenciling or artist's paint for each color to be stenciled, extender (optional), repositionable spray adhesive.

1

PLAN YOUR DESIGN.

Roll on base-coat paint; let dry. Plan where and how to apply the stencil. If you're applying a continuous border design, select a starting point for your design (a corner not seen from the room's entry is the best spot). For a ceiling-height stenciled border, use a carpenter's level, tape measure, and pencil to lightly mark dashes at a consistent height around the room.

2 PREPARE YOUR STENCIL.

Cut out the stencil design with a crafts knife, if necessary, and place the stencil facedown on a rag or piece of kraft paper. Spray a thin coat of repositionable spray adhesive onto the stencil back and allow it to set, per manufacturer's instructions. Some painters prefer using painter's tape around the stencil edges rather than spray adhesive to adhere stencils.

3 ATTACH THE STENCIL.

Press the sticky side of the stencil onto the surface. As you move the stencil later, wrap a clean, soft rag around your hands when you press on the stencil to ensure you don't apply any paint to the surface.

KEEP IT SIMPLE

You'll enjoy your stenciling treatment for years to come if you select simple, classic motifs and avoid using numerous high-contrast paint colors and specialty products. For example, basic fleur-de-lis, vines, florals, and architectural motifs work well with a variety of decorating styles. Also, apply stencils to areas where architectural molding traditionally occurs: at the ceiling line, at chair-rail height, and around windows and doors.

4 PREPARE PAINT PLATE.

Determine how many paint colors your stencil requires and prepare a divided plate or tray with the selected colors. Add a few drops of extender to each color to provide more time for working or blending paints. Mix extender and paint with a coffee stirrer or stick. Load an appropriately sized stencil brush with paint.

5 BLOT STENCIL BRUSH.

Tap the loaded stencil brush onto a piece of white paper or paper towel to remove excess paint and ensure even application.

MAKING STENCILS

You can transform most any simple image into a stencil. Place a photocopy of the image under a sheet of clear stencil film (available at crafts and paint stores) and trace the edges of the image with a fine-tip permanent marker. Cut out the shapes of your design with a crafts knife, working on a cutting mat. Be sure to label the front of your design.

Stenciled border *(continued)*

6 TAP ON STENCIL PAINT.

Dab the stencil brush into the appropriate areas of the stencil with a steady, circular motion, perpendicular to the wall. For a softer, more traditional look, dab the paint first and heaviest around the edge of the stencil; reload brush as necessary. Work paint toward the center of the area, blending for a smooth, consistent transition. Fill in all areas of the stencil where the first color appears.

7 TAP ON THE SECOND COLOR.

Load another stencil brush with the second color of paint and apply the paint to the appropriate sections of the stencil. Depending on the design of your stencil, you may need to apply a second layer of stencil film to the surface with each additional color. Follow your stencil manufacturer's instructions. Continue applying paint, using a different brush for each color.

8 CLEAN AND CONTINUE.

As soon as you're done applying paint, remove the stencil from the wall. Wipe off paint from the stencil with a clean, damp cloth. Reposition the clean stencil next to the completed design. If any paint seeps under the film while stenciling, allow the motif to dry and use a small artist's brush to touch up around the stencil with base-coat paint.

STENCILED RELIEF

S tenciled relief harkens to the intricate plasterwork and moldings that adorn the walls and ceilings of European sitting rooms, Gothic churches, and Victorian parlors. Master plaster artisans may require days and even months to layer on plaster details to create the appearance of thick, intricately carved moldings. But the simple yet effective technique described here uses only one layer of drywall compound.

Stenciled relief builds on the basic stenciling techniques outlined on pages 100–102. However, rather than applying paint within a stencil's cut-out areas, you apply a thin layer of drywall compound. Glaze over the relief adds contrast. The resulting effect combines the crispness of stenciling with depth and texture.

YOU'LL NEED

TIME: One day to apply treatment to 40 linear feet.

SKILLS: Working with drywall compound, brushing on glaze.

TOOLS: Foam or cloth roller, roller tray, stencil, crafts knife, painter's tape, small putty knife, butter knife, rags, mixing container, carpenter's level, pencil, tape measure.

MATERIALS: Drywall compound, glaze, latex paint.

SPREAD THE RELIEF

Don't limit stenciled relief to traditional ceiling-level borders and chair-rail placements. Use stencil relief around windows, doors, and arches to give these features architectural prominence. Apply stenciled relief to painted wood furniture—particularly doors, drawers, and trimwork—to give these pieces detailed finishing touches.

STENCIL A DISTINCTIVE TEXTURE.

Stenciled relief applied around a window frame acts almost like a part of the window treatment, enhancing the size and prominence of the window.

1 PREPARE STENCIL.

Roll on base-coat paint; let dry. Plan where and how to apply the stencil. Use a carpenter's level, tape measure, and pencil to lightly mark any necessary guidelines. If it is not precut, cut out the stencil design with a crafts knife. Position the stencil on the surface and secure it in place with repositionable spray adhesive or painter's tape.

Stenciled relief *(continued)*

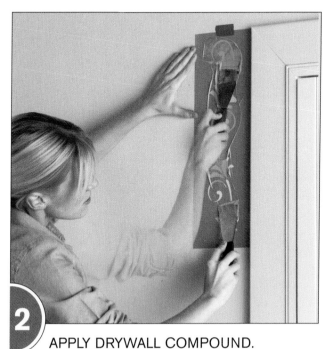

2 APPLY DRYWALL COMPOUND.

In a mixing container mix drywall compound per manufacturer's instructions, or use a premixed compound. Using a small putty knife, apply a ⅛- to ¼-inch-thick layer of compound over the entire stencil. Be careful not to push compound under the stencil while applying it.

3 REMOVE STENCIL.

Remove the stencil from the wall, pulling slowly and making sure compound adheres to the surface, rather than pulling away with the stencil.

4 FIX MISTAKES.

Touch up heavy or misshapen areas using a butter knife or putty knife wrapped in a thin, damp cloth. Allow compound to dry, following the manufacturer's instructions.

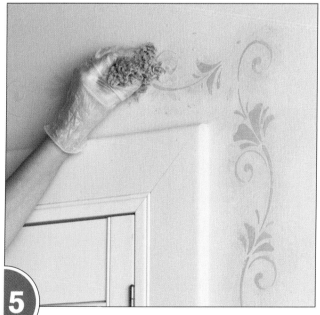

5 APPLY THE TOP-COAT GLAZE.

In a mixing container combine one part paint and two or three parts glaze; stir until blended. Form a damp rag into a soft pom-pom (see page 49) and load with glaze; blot off excess. Lightly rub glaze onto the surface in a loose, overlapping circular motion, allowing glaze to collect around relief edges. Turn to page 36 for more on glaze color washes.

WALLPAPER STENCILING

Wallpaper stenciling expands the size and scope of basic stenciling skills to cover larger surfaces. The technique allows you to create the look of delicately faded wallpaper with various top-coat glazes that blend or fade as you desire.

Look for wallpaper stencils at home centers, paint stores, and on the Internet. Because wallpaper stencils usually must be applied dozens of times to cover an entire wall or room, purchase at least two stencils of any design you select.

YOU'LL NEED

TIME: One to two days to apply treatment to a 400-square-foot area.

SKILLS: Working with stencils, mixing glazes.

TOOLS: Cloth or foam roller, roller tray, wallpaper stencil, painter's tape or repositionable spray adhesive, carpenter's level, stencil or thick chip brushes.

MATERIALS: Latex paint for base coat, metallic glaze, white or cream glaze, latex paints for top-coat stencil.

PLAN CAREFULLY

With wallpaper stencils, planning ahead is crucial. Before preparing any stencil paints, evaluate your stencil and see how it fits with the height and width of each wall. Purchase or make an additional stencil that you can cut to size to fit into corners and to go around doors and windows.

STENCIL ENTIRE WALLS.

Combine deep colors, metallic glazes, and large-scale classic stencils to simulate the look of rich, aged wallpaper.

Wallpaper stenciling *(continued)*

1 PLAN YOUR DESIGN.

Roll on base-coat paint; let dry. Plan how to apply your stencil to your walls. In general, start in a lower, inconspicuous corner and work up and over. (See "Plan Carefully" on page 105.) Spray repositionable adhesive or apply tape around the stencil, and press it onto the surface. Sweep a carpenter's level over the stencil to ensure that the stencil makes consistent contact.

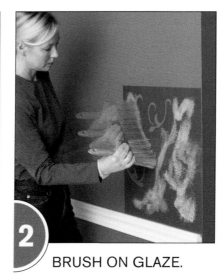

2 BRUSH ON GLAZE.

In separate containers, mix two colors of thin glaze (for our example, we used a metallic glaze and a creamy white accent glaze) by combining one part paint, two or three parts glaze, and one part water. Load a stencil brush or chip brush with the first glaze and dab glaze onto the stencil. Follow the general shape of the stencil, but allow portions of the base coat to appear through the glaze.

3 BRUSH ON THE ACCENT GLAZE.

While glaze is still wet, load a clean stencil brush or chip brush with the accent glaze and dab on areas of lighter glaze as a highlight. Allow glazes to blend in some areas.

4 BLEND AND SOFTEN.

Form a moistened cloth into a soft pom-pom (see page 49) and pounce on all areas of the stencil, blending the two glazes and softening the edges of stenciled areas.

5 CLEAN AND CONTINUE.

Lift the stencil and remove with one quick motion. If necessary, wipe off the back of the stencil. Reposition the stencil above or to the side of the finished section, carefully lining up the stencil to keep the pattern in register.

METALLIC LEAFING

Centuries ago, decorative painters attached flakes of actual gold, silver, and other precious metals to the architectural details of some of the world's most beautiful palaces and cathedrals.

You can achieve similar looks today by using metallic leafing kits, available at hobby and crafts stores. While kits typically don't contain precious metals, most kits provide you with squares of less expensive metallic foils that mirror the look of gold, silver, bronze, copper, or any of a host of other metals.

Because metal-leafing sheets can break, rip, and tarnish easily, always follow the manufacturer's instructions for handling them. In general, avoid touching the leaf directly with your fingers (the oils will tarnish the unsealed metal); use tissue, gloves, or tweezers to manipulate the sheets.

YOU'LL NEED

TIME: One day to apply 30 sheets of leafing.

SKILLS: Preparing surfaces for metallic leaf, applying metallic leaf, sealing surfaces.

TOOLS: Artist's brush, rags, tack cloth, fine-grit sandpaper, painter's tape, transparent tape.

MATERIALS: Metallic leaf sizing/adhesive, metallic leaf, latex paint for base coat, clear polyurethane.

ADD A REGAL TOUCH.

Gold leafing applied to a wide, richly detailed frame gives this inexpensive mirror the appearance of an ornate collector's item.

A LITTLE LEAFING HAS A LOT OF IMPACT

Use metallic leaf in small bursts for maximum impact.
Apply leafing to accent pieces, including frames, small tables, lamp bases, and decorative ledges. Or apply narrow strips and taped-off shapes of leafing as decorative borders and accents on larger wood furniture pieces, such as armoires, end tables, dining tables, and dressers.

CAUTION

Metallic leaf is extremely thin; even slight imperfections in a painted base coat will show through. Take the time to fully prepare the surface.

Metallic leafing *(continued)*

1 PREPARE THE SURFACE.

Brush or roll on a base coat of latex paint; let dry. If you plan to cover the entire project with leafing, use a medium tan, brown, or gray latex paint, because the base coat may show through portions of the leaf-covered surface. If you don't apply a base coat, apply a wood sealer to any bare wood or other porous surface.

2 SMOOTH THE SURFACE.

Leafing must be applied over a smooth surface, so rub the surface with a fine nylon finishing pad or very fine sandpaper. Wipe down the surface with a tack cloth.

3 APPLY THE SIZING.

Brush metallic leaf sizing onto the entire project surface with an artist's brush. Follow the manufacturer's recommendations for drying time. Sizing will generally change from milky to clear—an indication that it is ready for leaf application—in about an hour.

4 PRESS ON THE LEAF.

Separate one sheet of metallic leaf and its protective layer of tissue paper from the pad. Avoid touching the leaf; wear gloves or handle it with tweezers to prevent tarnishing. Apply the leaf to the surface, lightly pressing it into place by pressing on the tissue paper. Lift away the tissue paper, and brush away any flakes of metal leaf that didn't adhere to the surface.

5 APPLY THE NEXT SHEET OF LEAF.

Using the same technique, apply another sheet of metal leaf. For a consistently covered surface, overlap sheets of leaf slightly; for a more aged and rustic look, leave a slight space between applied areas.

6 RUB DOWN AND SEAL.

When you finish applying leaf to the entire project, use a clean, soft rag to lightly rub the surface and brush off any flakes that haven't adhered to the metallic leaf sizing. Brush on at least two coats of clear polyurethane or varnish to seal the project.

METALLIC GLAZING

Metallic glazing is a variation on other glazing techniques featured in this book. The difference is in the use of a metallic-color glaze rather than a pearlized, opalescent, creamy, or other tinted glaze product.

Formulations of metallic glazes simulate various metals' colors. Gold, silver, bronze, and copper glazes are commonly available, but you can find others. Like any glaze, you can apply a metallic glaze over a painted base coat by rolling on, sponging on, or using any other additive technique. You also can mix the glaze with paint to create a slightly metallic glaze.

Overall, the luster created with metallic glazes is not as shiny or deeply metallic as metal leafing (see page 107) or metal-rubbing (see page 111). However, for subtle shimmer that can enrich a wall or an entire room, metallic glazing is a good way to add some sparkle without overwhelming the eye.

YOU'LL NEED

TIME: One day to apply treatment to a 400-square-foot area.

SKILLS: Mixing glazes, applying glaze to surfaces.

TOOLS: Cloth or foam roller, roller tray, painter's tape, pencil, carpenter's level, plumb bob, tape measure, cheesecloth or soft rags.

MATERIALS: Metallic glaze, latex paint for base coat, latex paint for top coat (optional).

EMBOLDEN WITH SHINE AND SHIMMER.

Give any painted wall an instant dash of class by applying taped-off stripes of metallic glaze. For an even richer look, use both silver- and gold-based glazes on the same surface.

1 PLAN YOUR DESIGN.

Apply a base coat of latex paint to the surface; let dry. Using a carpenter's level, tape measure, pencil, and plumb bob, lay out a series of stripes and mark them with painter's tape. For additional information on taping designs, see pages 118–121.

2 APPLY SILVER GLAZE.

Pour silver metallic glaze into a shallow plate or tray. Dab a clean, moistened rag or piece of cheesecloth into the glaze. Blot off excess glaze on a piece of paper or clean rag. Glaze the stripe using any technique, such as those on pages 36, 44, and 48.

Metallic glazing *(continued)*

3 APPLY GOLD GLAZE.

Pour gold metallic glaze into another shallow plate or tray. Dab another clean, moistened rag into the glaze and blot off excess. Wipe, drag, or rag on the gold glaze within another taped-off space. Continue applying glaze to various taped-off areas.

4 LET DRY AND TOUCH UP.

After metallic glazes are applied, carefully remove tape. Touch up any edges with a scrap of cloth to apply metallic glaze, or an artist's brush to apply the base-coat paint.

CHOOSING BETWEEN SILVER AND GOLD

Although you may prefer silver or gold decorative accents, this preference does not need to carry over into your choice of metallic glazes. While warm colors mix well with gold metallic glaze and cool colors blend nicely with silver glaze, you can blend just about any paint color with either metallic glaze—often to a surprisingly attractive effect.

A base coat of flat, light yellow latex paint.

Yellow paint mixed with gold glaze and then applied to a surface.

Yellow paint mixed with silver glaze and then applied to a surface.

Gilding and metal rubbing offer some of the best aspects of other metallic techniques featured in this book. Like metallic leafing (see page 107), you can apply a significant amount of metal particles to a surface, producing a shinier, richer effect than metallic glazes. And like metallic glazes, gilding is an easy glaze-based process that goes on more quickly than working with delicate sheets of metal leafing.

Gilding is a particularly strong treatment when covering intricately detailed surfaces, including trimwork, molding, and plaster medallions. With proper surface preparation, gilding also can work well on molded foam, plastic, and metal surfaces.

YOU'LL NEED

TIME: Half a day to gild a medium-size project.

SKILLS: Mixing glaze, rubbing on glaze.

TOOLS: Mixing container, paint mitt (optional), 3-inch brush, stencil or chip brush, rags.

MATERIALS: Latex primer (if necessary), light or medium latex paint for base coat, dark latex paint, metallic glaze, extender.

EXTENDER ADDS TIME

Adding latex paint extender to your top-coat glaze gives more time to rub and work the finish. (The amount to add may be a few drops or a few teaspoons—refer to the manufacturer's instructions.) You can buy extenders at paint and crafts stores.

RUB ON METALLIC SHINE.

Update an old light fixture (this one was antique brass) by rubbing on a two-toned metallic-silver finish.

Gilding and metal-rubbing *(continued)*

1 PREPARE YOUR SURFACE.

Prepare the surface to be gilded. Rub metal and glossy plastic surfaces with a fine nylon abrasive pad to dull the shiny top coat. Sand wood surfaces with fine-grit sandpaper. Wipe sanded surfaces with a tack cloth.

2 APPLY THE BASE COAT.

Brush or wipe on a latex paint base coat. Use a brush, paint mitt, or other tool to fully cover the surface. Metal and plastic surfaces require a coat of special primer (available at home centers and paint stores), followed by a coat of the latex base coat. Let the base coat dry.

CAUTION

Although gilding is more durable than metallic leafing, avoid applying the treatment to high-use fixtures, such as sinks, faucets, or doorknobs and handles. To increase the longevity of gilded finishes, apply at least two coats of clear polyurethane over the completed finish. Glossy, clear polyurethane gives a shiny surface; a satin or matte finish adds a less lustrous surface. Clean gilded surfaces with a soft cloth and mild, soapy water. Avoid using cleaners with harsh abrasives or bleach.

3 PREPARE TOP-COAT GLAZE.

In a plastic container, mix one part metallic glaze and three parts medium-tone latex paint; stir until blended. Test the glaze on a sample board for desired metallic sheen; add more metallic glaze, if necessary. Load a moistened rag or old stencil brush with metallic glaze and press the glaze into all cracks and crevices of the surface.

4 SPREAD THE TOP-COAT GLAZE.

Using a soft 3-inch brush, spread out the glaze from the paint-saturated cracks and crevices, creating an even coat. If the glaze dries while brushing out, apply more glaze and add several drops of extender.

5 BUFF AND REMOVE EXCESS GLAZE.

While the glaze is still wet, use a soft cloth to rub glaze from high spots and flat areas of the surface. Allow the lighter base coat to be fully exposed in the highest spots. Apply two coats of polyurethane to the surface.

COLOR COMBOS FOR OTHER METALS

By modifying the paint colors you choose, you can use the gilding technique described here to simulate a wide range of metals. Refer to the paint recipes to the right for paint combinations that replicate specific metals. Be sure to test all gilding treatments on a sample board before applying to the actual item or surface.

Metal/Effect	Latex paint for base coat	Top coat(s)
Aged bronze	Golden yellow	Copper latex paint + metallic glaze
		Dark brown latex paint
Antique silver	Light gray	Medium gray latex paint + metallic glaze
Antique gold	Light gold	Medium gold latex paint + metallic glaze
Brass	Medium gold	Dark gold latex paint + metallic glaze
Pewter	Medium gray	Dark gray latex paint + metallic glaze
		Black latex paint
Steel	Light gray	Dark gray latex paint
Rusted iron	Medium brown	Dark brown latex paint
		Black latex paint

WEATHERED COPPER

Weathered copper, or verdigris, results from chemical reactions that copper metal undergoes when exposed to rain and atmospheric elements. Rather than relying on time and weather to age expensive copper items, you can quickly simulate the look with this decorative paint treatment. And unlike actual verdigris, the paint treatment allows you to control where and how intensely the weathering occurs on your projects.

Weathered copper paint finishes fit into a wide range of decorating styles. Country, cottage, classical, and even contemporary projects all take on a warm yet timeworn glow. Like other metallic finishes featured in this book, weathered copper can be applied to practically any surface. Plastic, ceramic, terra cotta, and wood surfaces can be painted and glazed to give the appearance of being crafted or covered in copper metal.

WARM UP WITH WEATHERED COPPER.

Apply a weathered copper paint treatment to a classically shaped ceramic or plastic urn to create an inexpensive planter with the appearance of metal that has spent years outdoors.

YOU'LL NEED

TIME: Half to one day to apply treatment to a medium-size project.

SKILLS: Mixing glazes, working with a verdigris tool.

TOOLS: 3-inch brush, mixing container, chip brush, duct tape, hook-and-loop tape, spray bottle.

MATERIALS: Copper-color latex paint for base coat, two or three small tubes of turquoise artist's acrylic paint, glaze.

COUNT ON COPPER AS AN ACCENT

Like most metallic paint treatments, weathered copper is most effective in small doses. Use it on small furniture, such as a plant stand or side table, and on accent items, such as urns, pots, sculptures, and trellises.

1

PREPARE YOUR SURFACE.

Rub metal and glossy plastic surfaces with a fine-nylon abrasive pad. Sand wood surfaces with fine-grit sandpaper. Prime metal and plastic surfaces with appropriate products. Brush on the copper base coat with overlapping strokes to heighten the appearance and texture of weathered metal. Let the base coat dry.

2

BUY OR MAKE A VERDIGRIS TOOL.

Purchase a verdigris tool (available at most crafts or hobby stores) or make your own. Trim the bristles from a 2- or 3-inch chip brush and wrap the soft side of a strip of hook-and-loop fastener tape around the chip brush. Secure it with duct tape. Use scissors to cut the hook-and-loop tape into several vertical strips.

3

WET THE SURFACE.

Fill a clean hand sprayer with water and mist the base-coated surface to wet it slightly.

4

PREPARE THE VERDIGRIS GLAZES.

In a shallow paint plate or tray, mix one part acrylic artist's paint with one part glaze for each verdigris color. Load the verdigris tool with glaze and blot it on paper or a clean rag. Smear, pat, tap, and dab the glaze onto the surface in a random and uneven motion. Load the same verdigris brush with another color of glaze, blot, and apply to the surface.

5

FIX ANY FAULTS.

If you apply glaze too thickly, spray the area with a fine mist of water and then dab out the overly glazed portion to reveal more base coat. When you are satisfied with the appearance, let the project dry; then apply two coats of polyurethane to seal the treatment.

SOUTHWESTERN FRESCO

This technique, which gives the look of thick walls of mud and straw, takes its name from the texture and color of centuries-old adobe walls found throughout the American Southwest. The southwestern fresco technique requires only one thin coat of drywall compound and three colors of latex paint.

The finished technique is dramatic and rustic. Apply it to large spaces or as an accent for a single focal wall. The technique looks especially attractive on arched architectural features, such as entryways, pass-throughs, and wall niches.

YOU'LL NEED

TIME: One to two days to apply treatment to a 400-square-foot area.

SKILLS: Mixing paint and drywall compound, applying compound to walls.

TOOLS: 6-inch drywall knife, drywall pan, stir stick, foam roller, roller tray.

MATERIALS: Matte-finish polyurethane, drywall compound, three colors of latex paint.

PICK NATURAL COLORS

The southwestern fresco technique looks best when the three colors of latex paint suggest actual adobe wall colors. To achieve an appropriate level of contrast, select three shades of warm gray, golden beige, or rusty orange that appear at the same level on three neighboring paint strips. Also, select fairly dark colors on the paint strips (probably the second-from-the-bottom color options), because mixing paint and compound creates a lighter color.

SPREAD ON RICH TEXTURE.

Give flat drywall a rustic texture and rich color by using a drywall knife to spread on a layer of slightly mixed drywall compound and latex paint.

LET COLORS BLEND ON THE WALL

Don't overmix the three paint colors into the drywall compound in the drywall pan. Most of the color blending in this technique happens as you trowel on the plaster and paint to the wall.

1 PREPARE DRYWALL COMPOUND.

Prime-paint the surface and let dry. If using powdered drywall compound, mix it according to the manufacturer's directions. Fill a drywall trough with approximately three parts wet drywall compound. Pour in one part each of three different colors of latex paint. The ratio of total paint to compound is approximately 1:1.

2 MIX PAINT AND COMPOUND.

Lightly mix the paint and drywall compound, stirring with a paint stick. Mix three separate batches of compound and paint in the tray. Avoid overblending colors; after mixing you should still see three distinct colors within the compound tray.

3 SPREAD ON COMPOUND.

Starting high and in a corner, spread on tinted compound with a 6-inch drywall knife. Apply compound in a downward motion. As you drag the knife down, occasionally flick your wrist to each side, creating jagged edges. Allow colors to blend, but don't overblend. Continue spreading on compound in vertical strips to the side and below the completed area.

4 REFINE YOUR WORK.

Step back 8 to 10 feet and evaluate coverage and mix of paint and compound. While the compound is still wet, spread on small amounts of tinted compound to areas that need more color and/or texture. Allow the compound to dry overnight; open windows and doors to increase ventilation. Use a small foam roller to roll on a coat of matte polyurethane to seal and protect the surface.

STRIPES

The decorative effects you can achieve when you combine latex paint and painter's tape are limited only by your imagination.

For consistent, regularly spaced stripes, use measuring tools and a carpenter's level to help guide placement of the tape. Mark all measurements for your design on the wall before you begin taping. For a more casual look, space the tape lines without measuring, varying thin and wide bands. But a carpenter's level is essential to ensuring that the tape lines are applied straight and true.

The direction of the stripes affects the look of your design. Vertical stripes visually lift a ceiling and make a space seem taller. Horizontal stripes visually expand a room and make it seem wider. Diagonal stripes give walls a dynamic sense by leading the eye in the direction the stripes flow.

YOU'LL NEED

TIME: One to two days to apply treatment to a 400-square-foot area.

SKILLS: Planning designs, applying tape, rolling on paint.

TOOLS: Tape measure, graph paper, color pencils, carpenter's level, plumb bob, painter's tape (in various widths), cloth or foam rollers, roller trays, paintbrushes.

MATERIALS: Several colors of latex paint, as required for your design (we applied two shades of light green to light yellow base coat).

GENERATE GRAPHIC APPEAL.

Horizontal bands of contrasting paint can visually widen a space. Here, sage-green bands of paint on a beige background give this living room wall visual attitude and rhythm.

PAINT SHEENS ENHANCE EFFECT

For a more subtle taped-off look, pair semigloss with flat sheens of the same paint color. Or pair a satin wall color and a glaze mixture (metallic glaze and the same satin wall color).

1 PLAN YOUR DESIGN.

Plan the design for your stripes before beginning to apply tape or paint. Take accurate measurements of the wall or space to be painted. Use graph paper and color pencils to draw a scale version of the design.

2 MEASURE AND MARK THE WALL.

Roll on base-coat paint and let dry. For horizontal stripes, use a tape measure to lay out dimensions of the stripes. Use a carpenter's level and appropriate color pencils to draw lines on the wall. For vertical stripes, use a tape measure and a plumb bob to lay out the stripes.

▼ CAUTION

Use painter's tape—not masking tape—when you lay out your striped wall designs. Masking tape is more likely to remove base-coat paint when it's peeled off. Painter's tape seals down tighter along the edges too, which keeps paint from bleeding under it. This makes it easier to get a sharp edge on your stripes.

3 APPLY TAPE.

Using pencil lines as a guide, apply painter's tape on the outside edge of each band to be painted with your first accent color. Burnish the tape edge with a plastic tool or your fingernail to seal it tightly to the wall. Apply a small X with tape in the areas that won't be painted.

4 APPLY PAINT.

Brush or roll on the first paint color in the appropriate area. Apply a second coat, if necessary. Carefully remove the tape as soon as the final coat of paint is applied. Remove tape markers in unpainted areas. Let the paint dry.

5 CONTINUE PAINTING.

Apply and burnish tape on the outside edges of each band to be painted with the second accent color. Brush or roll on the second paint color to the appropriate areas, then remove the tape. Let the paint dry.

TAPE GRIDS

Like tape stripes (see page 118), tape grids offer a wealth of design options, require few special tools, and look dramatic.

Tape grids require a bit more planning than tape stripes. Experiment with the size and shape of the paintable space before you begin applying paint. (To ensure you achieve the desired proportions, draw your design to scale on graph paper before taping.) Smaller squares enable you to incorporate more paint colors and give a more graphic or formal attitude. Large squares (2×2 feet and larger) have a looser feel. And don't limit yourself to only squares: Rectangles combined in different heights and widths can create the illusion of architectural moldings or paneled walls.

You can fill in the spaces in your design with solid-color latex paint, a decorative paint treatment, or a combination of treatments.

YOU'LL NEED

TIME: One to two days to apply treatment to a 400-square-foot area.

SKILLS: Planning a design, applying tape, rolling on paint.

TOOLS: Tape measure, graph paper, color pencils, carpenter's level, plumb bob, painter's tape (in various widths), cloth or foam rollers, roller trays, paintbrushes.

MATERIALS: Several colors of latex paint, as required for your design (we applied bright green and three shades of purple to a light gray base coat).

CHECK THE WALLS.

A tape grid of colorful blocks is perfect for a child's bedroom. Multiple contrasting colors can be combined in one treatment.

GRID PULLS A ROOM TOGETHER

Use a tape grid when your room has several important colors that don't mix well in a blending-focused technique, like sponging or ragging on. (For example, blending complementary colors, such as yellow and purple, can result in a muddy gray or brown.) Create a tape grid with enough spaces to allow each color to be applied evenly throughout the room.

1 LAY OUT THE VERTICAL LINES.

Roll on base-coat paint and let dry. Use a tape measure, plumb bob, and carpenter's level to mark the spacing for the vertical lines. (The lines in this design are 12 inches apart.) Apply painter's tape to the wall along the lines. Press down the tape with a burnishing tool or fingernail to adhere it tightly to the wall.

2 ADD THE HORIZONTAL LINES.

Using a tape measure and carpenter's level, mark off the spacing for the horizontal lines. (The horizontal lines in this design also are 12 inches apart.) Apply the tape and burnish. Make sure it adheres well where it overlaps.

3 PICK AND PLAN THE COLORS.

Open all the colors of paint you plan to use in the treatment. Mix any glazes required for your treatment. Using a small brush, place a dot of the appropriate paint color or glaze in a corner of each block. Step back and make sure the arrangement is balanced and appealing.

4 APPLY THE PAINTS.

Roll or brush on the first color of paint, or apply the first decorative paint finish. Use new or clean tools to apply additional colors or finishes. Remove the tape as soon as the final paint or finish is applied.

STAMPING

Stamping, like stenciling, enables you to produce crisp, graphic images on walls, furniture, and other surfaces. Generally stamping is quicker and easier than stenciling, because you simply stamp an image on the surface rather than having to repeatedly clean and reposition a stencil.

In recent years, the popularity of stamping has grown immensely. You can find decorative painting stamps at hobby, crafts, and paint stores in a variety of designs. Be sure you purchase foam stamps that can absorb latex paint; avoid the more delicate rubber stamps that are designed for ink and paper projects.

YOU'LL NEED

TIME: One day to apply treatment to 40 linear feet.

SKILLS: Planning a design, working with decorative stamps.

TOOLS: Roller, roller tray, tape measure, graph paper, color pencils, carpenter's level, rubber gloves, painter's tape, paintbrushes, stamps, artist's brushes.

MATERIALS: Several colors of latex paint, as required for your design (we applied three bright colors on a cream base coat).

RELOADING THE STAMP

For crisp edges and solid color, load the stamp with paint after you stamp each impression. For a more casual look and slightly transparent color, reload the stamp with paint every other or every third time you stamp.

FAST, FAST, FAST RESULTS.

Quickly give any wall the appearance of a wallpaper border by combining a taped horizontal band of paint and various stamps in coordinating styles and colors.

1 MEASURE AND MARK OFF.

Apply base-coat paint to wall. Let dry. Use a tape measure and carpenter's level to mark off a horizontal band and apply painter's tape. (The width of this border was determined by adding 3 inches of border on either side of the tallest point of the stamped design.) Roll on base-coat paint for the border background using a foam roller. Let the paint dry.

2 PLAN YOUR DESIGN.

Plan how you want to place the stamps on the painted horizontal band. You can use a single stamp or combine multiple stamps. You can stamp images in a consistent, regular pattern, or stamp images in a free-form manner. Use appropriate color pencils to mark any guide points you need for stamp placement.

3 PREPARE THE STAMP.

Pour each color of paint into a shallow plate or tray. Dab the stamp into the appropriate color of paint or use a small brush to apply paint directly to the stamp.

CUSTOM STAMPS

If you can't find decorative stamps that appeal to you at crafts and paint stores, make them yourself. Purchase sheets of tightly pored ¼- to ⅜-inch-thick foam from a crafts or hobby store. (For a more rustic stamped image, use cellulose sponge or thin insulation foam.) Draw a simple shape or design on the foam sheet with a permanent marker. Use a crafts knife or sharp scissors to cut out your design. Glue the foam pieces to a small block of wood, using non-water based glue. Let dry.

4 BLOT OFF EXCESS.

Press the stamp lightly onto a piece of cardboard or paper to remove excess paint. Leave enough paint on the stamp to make a solid image.

5 STAMP THE IMAGE.

Position the stamp and press it firmly straight onto the surface. Lift the stamp. Load stamp with paint, blot, and continue stamping the surface. After the stamped images dry, use an artist's brush to fill in any unstamped portions of the design and make stamp edges crisp and consistent.

STAMPED WALLPAPER

Instead of merely stamping on a decorative border, you can stamp randomly all over a wall to create the appearance of custom wallpaper. Use simple stamps and more subtle, lower contrast paints. Test-stamp the proposed pattern on a large sheet of cardboard or paper and tape it to the wall to see if you like the result.

TEXTURED IMPRINTING

This technique combines aspects of fresco techniques (see pages 67 and 116) with stamping (see page 122). Textured imprinting enables you to produce a unique finish: You choose the thickness of the coat of drywall compound, the items to be pressed into the wet compound, and the spacing of the impressions. Topping off the dried surface with a coat of glaze or paint gives you even more opportunity to customize the look.

YOU'LL NEED

TIME: One day to apply treatment to a 400-square-foot area.

SKILLS: Applying drywall compound, making imprints, working with glaze.

TOOLS: Drywall trough, 6-inch drywall knife, various plastic or silk leaves, pan, tweezers (optional), rags, mixing containers.

MATERIALS: Drywall compound, glaze, latex paint.

IMPRINT IDEAS

You can use any flat, water-resistant items to create impressions with this technique. Try using old printing blocks, die-cut wood shapes, sculptured wood trim, metal stencils, coins, rustic woodworking tools, or even gears.

LAYER ON TEXTURE.

Give walls a custom texture by pressing plastic or silk leaves of various distinctive species—maple, oak, and ash all work well—into still-wet drywall compound.

1

SPREAD ON DRYWALL COMPOUND.

Prime the surface and let dry. If you're using powdered drywall compound, mix the compound according to the manufacturer's instructions. Fill a drywall trough with compound, and apply it to the wall with a 6-inch drywall knife. Apply it with long downward strokes in a layer about ¼ inch thick.

2 PREPARE THE LEAVES.

Fill a shallow pan with water. Remove several leaves from plastic or silk plants. Dip a leaf into the water and wet both sides. Shake excess water from the leaf.

3 MAKE LEAF IMPRESSIONS.

Press the moist leaf into the still-wet drywall compound. Lightly press over the entire leaf, making a consistent impression, including veins, texture, and shape.

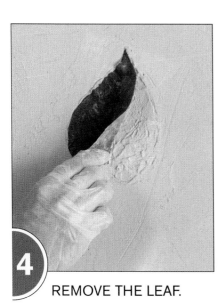

4 REMOVE THE LEAF.

Use fingernails (or tweezers, if necessary) to gently lift the leaf from the plaster. If the imprint is inconsistent or too faint, place the leaf over the partial impression and press on areas of the leaf where additional detail is required. To eliminate an impression, press a moist rag over the impression, trowel on a thin coat of additional compound, and then press another leaf.

5 APPLY A GLAZE TOP COAT.

Let the compound dry completely. In a plastic container combine one part glaze and one part latex paint; mix thoroughly. Wipe on the glaze color wash in a broad, circular motion, using a rag or mitt. See page 36 for more about applying a color wash.

▼ CAUTION

As drywall compound dries, it releases water that's been mixed in with the compound. Applying a ⅛- to ¼-inch layer of drywall compound to an entire room produces a great deal of moisture. Weather permitting, open windows and doors and set up a fan to aid in drying. If drying is a concern, consider applying drywall to one wall at a time. If the drywall compound cracks while drying, you're applying the compound too thickly and possibly forcing the compound to dry too quickly. Repair any cracks (see page 144 for help) and allow repairs to dry more slowly.

Also, dried compound produces a lot of dust and will brush off on hands and clothing. Apply at least two coats of paint or glaze to seal.

VENETIAN PLASTER

Venetian plaster has quickly become one of the most in-demand decorative wall treatments. Venetian plaster's combination of satin-smooth finish and deep, semitransparent color makes it a finish that is at once Old World yet completely modern. Professional Venetian plaster artisans are few and often quite expensive. While the technique does take some practice to apply well, the final results can be stunning.

Traditional Venetian plaster requires numerous thin coats of tinted plaster, but specialty products enable you to create an effect similar to real Venetian plaster in only two coats. (You can find these products on the Internet and at most home centers and paint stores). Premixed products typically come tinted in a range of popular colors. You can add additional latex paint or universal tints to tweak the hue to your liking.

YOU'LL NEED

TIME: One to two days to apply treatment to a 400-square-foot area.

SKILLS: Finishing drywall, rolling on paint, spreading Venetian plaster.

TOOLS: Sandpaper, roller, roller tray, mixing containers, steel Venetian plaster spatulas (3- and 6-inch), plaster trough, rags, rubber gloves, small chip brush.

MATERIALS: Latex paint for base coat, Venetian plaster compound, clear top coat/ polyurethane appropriate for Venetian plaster.

OLD WORLD COLOR AND TEXTURE.

A light blue base coat combined with two layers of light gray Venetian plaster gives walls an aged luster. Burnishing the top coat gives the surface an even deeper shine.

1 PREPARE TO PLASTER.

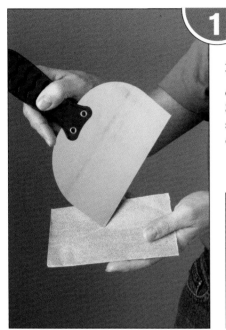

Apply primer and base coat. Let dry. Wipe the surface with a rag or tack cloth to ensure a smooth surface. Sand one edge of a 6-inch steel spatula to apply plaster with an extremely smooth finish.

PRACTICE FIRST

Practice the Venetian plaster technique on sample boards before trying it on an actual wall. As you practice, you'll discover your style and intensity for applying the plaster. See page 41 for more information about sample boards.

▼ CAUTION

Venetian plaster requires a smooth or very lightly textured base surface. Take time to fully prepare all surfaces, including repairing cracks and holes, sanding smooth, and priming prior to beginning this decorative treatment.

2 READY THE PLASTER.

Fill a plaster trough with a small amount of Venetian plaster. (Venetian plaster dries quickly, so keep only a small amount in the trough.) Apply plaster, thinned with a small amount of water, if needed, into corners and along the ceiling line with a spatula or a small chip brush.

3 LOAD THE SPATULA.

Load a 6-inch spatula with a small amount of plaster and begin spreading plaster on the wall. To control the amount of plaster you load on the spatula, use a plastic spoon or a 3-inch spatula. Start high in a corner, working the plaster into the wall.

Venetian plaster *(continued)*

4 SPREAD THE PLASTER.

As you apply the plaster to the wall, hold the spatula at a low angle to lay a thin coat on the wall. Spread the plaster over a 2-foot-square section with a consistent diagonal motion.

5 REFINE THE PLASTER.

While the plaster is still wet, scrape back over it with the spatula held at a higher angle. Remove excess plaster, leaving only a thin coat of plaster on the wall. Apply plaster to another 2-foot-square section, working down and across the surface. Follow the manufacturer's recommendations for drying time.

6 BACK-BURNISH PLASTER.

After the first coat of plaster has dried, back-burnish the surface by running a clean 6-inch spatula held at a high angle over the surface to remove any raised bits of plaster.

CAUTION

PUT PLASTER OVER CLEAN WALLS

Venetian plaster is very thin and will allow any discoloration, pencil marks, or paint to show through. Always prime and base-coat walls before applying a coat of plaster. Cracks and flaws in the walls could also mar the finished surface.

SMOOTH TOOLS ARE ESSENTIAL

Venetian plaster requires smooth, clean spatulas. Wipe off spatulas frequently with a damp cloth. Between coats wash spatulas thoroughly in soapy water. Use fine-gauge steel wool and fine-grit sandpaper to keep the spatulas in exceptional condition.

7 APPLY THE SECOND LAYER.

Apply a second layer of plaster using the technique previously described. Fill in areas where plaster was applied too thin. Create consistent plaster coverage over the surface. Let the plaster dry.

8 BACK-BURNISH AGAIN.

Back-burnish the second coat of plaster to remove high particles of plaster. If necessary, apply a third coat to areas where color and texture seem too thin. Let dry.

9 EVALUATE THE RESULTS.

Evaluate the completely dry surface. Fill in any remaining thin or bare patches with a 3-inch spatula, using the technique previously described. Let dry.

10 SEAL AND PROTECT.

Apply an acrylic or polyurethane top coat designed for use with Venetian plaster. Most acrylic top coats are spread on with the 6-inch spatula, using the same motion you used to apply the plaster. Follow manufacturer's instructions.

Tools
AND MATERIALS

As decorative painting has gained popularity, high-quality tools and materials have become easier to find. Most of the supplies you need to create stunning decorative treatments are available at home centers, paint stores, crafts stores, and discount stores. Internet resources and retailers offer easy access to specialty products that only a few years ago would have been difficult for the average do-it-yourselfer to locate.

All these decorative painting products make it easy to spend a small fortune on gadgets and painting supplies. To help you figure out how to spend your decorative painting budget wisely, the following pages feature recommendations for the most important and versatile tools.

You rarely need to scrimp or splurge on decorative painting supplies. Buy good-quality tools and durable materials whenever you have a choice, but realize that the highest-priced products are not always necessary to achieve professional-looking results. Build your collection of decorative painting tools and supplies gradually, as you work on specific projects or treatments. You're more likely to reuse tools and paint-and-glaze combinations that you're experienced with and that offer reliable results.

STANDARD PAINT TOOLS

Decorative painting effects all start with surface preparation, priming, and base coating. These tasks call for the tools and supplies you would use to paint any room.

SPECIALTY TOOLS

A few specialty tools are necessary to get the desired results. This section will help you separate the must-have decorative painting tools from the nonessential.

DECORATIVE STANDBYS

You'll use some decorative painting tools in dozens of different paint treatments. For frequently used tools purchase high-quality items that you can wash and reuse for multiple projects and techniques.

All paint projects require some basic tools. You probably have some of them already. While you don't need to own every item described here, you likely will need most of them at some point.

In addition to an assortment of brushes and roller covers (see page 133), disposable **paint pads** can speed up the application of a base coat. Look for pads in a variety of sizes, naps, and shapes. Corner pads are especially helpful for simultaneously painting a smooth line of paint on walls that meet in a corner.

Include an assortment of mixing tools in your kit. Clean out a variety of food containers or purchase inexpensive **plastic buckets** ranging in size from one quart to five gallons. A **metal paint can opener** is an essential—and usually free—tool to open paint cans easily and without ruining the lid. **Plastic pour spouts** clip onto standard gallon cans of paint and enable easy pouring. **Mixing paddles** attach to an electric hand drill and let you quickly mix custom glazes and paint colors.

Rolling on paint requires several tools, including appropriate-size metal roller frames and sloped plastic or metal **roller pans** that help you load the roller cover with paint and squeeze out the excess. Inexpensive plastic roller-pan liners let you quickly clean out trays and switch paints. A **roller grid** that slips into a standard five-gallon bucket is a handy addition when rolling on a room's worth of paint. An **extension pole** that screws onto the end of a standard roller frame helps you paint a ceiling or tall wall without mounting a stepladder. You also can cover more surface area while standing in one place by using an extension pole.

To make cleanup go more quickly, have a variety of **lint-free cotton rags** on hand. Use old T-shirts or towels, or purchase a box of paint rags at a home center. While painting, always have several moist rags close at hand to clean up spills and splatters. A **stainless steel wire brush** is handy for cleaning dried paint from the upper portions of paintbrushes. A **5-in-1 tool** works especially well to scrape still-wet paint from roller covers and open paint cans, among other tasks. A **brush and roller spinner** is useful when you need to quickly wash and dry your tools and use them with different paint or for another project.

Paint can opener

5-in-1 tool

1-quart bucket

Mixing paddle (attaches to a drill)

Roller pan liner

Stainless-steel wire brush

Roller pan

Pour spouts for gallon can

Rags (lint-free cotton)

Roller grid for 5-gallon bucket

5-gallon bucket

Paint pads

Brushes and Roller Covers

Synthetic bristle brush
Use synthetic bristle brushes with latex and water-base paints.

Natural bristle brush
Use natural-bristle brushes with oil-base paints.

1-inch brush
Apply paint in tight places and on delicate trim work with a 1-inch brush.

2- to 3-inch trim brush
(Angled preferably)
Use angled 1½- to 3-inch trim brushes to paint moldings

4- to 5-inch brush
(flat preferably)
A 4- or 5-inch flat-ended brush is great to paint larger surfaces quickly and to paint along the ceiling and floor line in preparation for rolling.

Foam roller
Disposable foam roller covers apply paint with a flat, level texture.

Longer-nap roller
Longer-nap roller covers are ideal for textured surfaces and areas that absorb a lot of paint.

Standard 9-inch roller
A standard 9-inch roller applies paint quickly and effectively.

Short-nap roller
Short-nap roller covers give paint a lightly textured, or orange-peel, finish.

3-inch wide roller
Narrow rollers reach into tight spaces and are ideal for rolling paint onto smaller areas.

Before diving into any decorative painting project, take the time to prepare the surfaces you'll paint and the room in which you'll work. While preparation work is never as gratifying as working with paints and glazes, your finished projects turn out better if you take time and utilize the following prep tools.

To clean a surface before applying any paint, wipe it down with soap and water or a solution of diluted **TSP (trisodium phosphate).** TSP is available premixed or as powder that you mix to the desired concentration. Use clean **sponges or rags** to wash down your surfaces. Have a pair of stepladders—a **3- or 4-foot ladder** and a **6-foot ladder**—on hand to help you safely and comfortably paint ceilings and walls in rooms with standard 8-foot ceilings. Know how your ladders lock open and avoid stepping on the top step while working.

Fill any minor holes or cracks with **spackling compound**; fill larger holes and cracks with **joint or drywall compound.** Apply compounds with a **3-inch putty knife** and then sand the dried compound with a **rubber sanding block** and an assortment of **sandpapers**, including medium, fine, and very fine grits.

Take the time to completely mask the floor, trim, and other surfaces that you aren't painting. **Canvas drop cloths** are the traditional cover for floors, but they're heavy, costly, and permeable to large spills. **Paper or plastic-lined paper drop cloths** are a relatively inexpensive and disposable choice to protect floors; they're available in rolls or individual sheets. **Plastic sheeting** can be used as a floor cloth as well, although plastic can be dangerously slippery when water or paint spills. Apply **painter's tape** (not white or cream masking tape) around the edges of all baseboards, window and door frames, and other moldings.

Use blue painter's tape for latex paint projects; green for oil-base projects. Look for tape in widths ranging from ½ to 3 inches as well as in special formulas for adhering to glass and metal surfaces. You also can use painter's tape to secure drop cloths.

Protect yourself with old, comfortable clothes that you don't mind ruining, or purchase a pair of canvas **painter's coveralls,** overalls, or pants available in a range of sizes and styles. Paper ones are also available. A **painter's cap** with a small brim protects your hair from paint splatters and helps shield your eyes and face. Although latex paint is relatively fume-free, wear a **sanding and painting mask** while sanding any surfaces, painting in confined spaces, or if you're sensitive to fumes or dust. If you're working with oil-base paints or more toxic cleaners, upgrade to a **respirator mask.**

GOOD PREP EASES JOB

If you do a thorough job preparing to paint, actually applying the paint to the project or room goes more quickly and smoothly. For detailed instructions on painting prep techniques, see page 148.

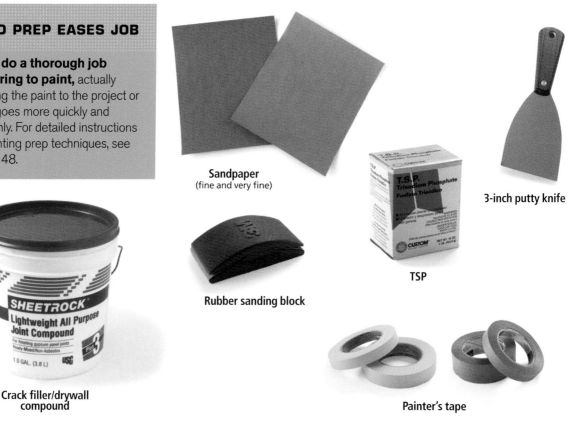

Sandpaper
(fine and very fine)

Rubber sanding block

TSP

3-inch putty knife

Crack filler/drywall compound

Painter's tape

Painter's cap

Plastic sheeting

Roll of kraft paper

Sanding and painting masks

Canvas drop cloth

Painter's coveralls

Stepladders
(4-ft and 6-ft)

PAINTING TOOLS

Essential decorative painting tools are few and surprisingly simple. Because you're more likely to use these items for multiple techniques, choose good-quality versions and thoroughly clean them when you're done using them.

Build up a collection of sponges to perform a host of decorative painting tasks. Thick, tight-pore **cellulose sponges** (3 to 4 inches thick) are ideal for washing on a coat of thinned paint, whitewash, or glaze. Cellulose sponges are generally cheaper, larger, and more durable than sea sponges. However, natural **sea sponges** are necessary when applying treatments where texture is important. Sea sponges come in various shapes, sizes, and species; select one or two sea sponges that you can hold comfortably in one hand and that have appealing texture. Thin, rectangular **kitchen sponges**

generally have undesirable texture to use as painting tools. You should keep a few close at hand to quickly clean up spills, however.

While you can use old T-shirts and towels for decorative painting, clean, lint-free cotton cloths are worth purchasing new. **Chamois cloth,** sometimes labeled as "suede cloth" or "sueded cotton," is thick, absorbent, and produces a rich, soft texture when used an applicator tool. **Terry cloth** comes in a variety of weaves and absorbencies; its looped surface produces a slightly rough texture. **Cheesecloth** can range from smooth, thin cotton sheeting to roughly woven poly-cotton blends. Also, new or used **paper** or **plastic bags, newspaper,** and **kraft paper** can all be used to add or remove decorative finishes for walls and other surfaces.

Many decorative painting techniques—such as strips, grids, stenciling, and borders—require careful planning, measuring, and marking of guidelines. Use **metal tape measures** or **rulers** to indicate specific measurements; cloth tape measures can stretch or wrinkle and result in inaccurate measurements. Use **metal straightedges** or a **4-foot carpenter's level** to help draw straight lines. Carpenter's levels have the additional benefit of helping you draw level horizontal lines and plumb vertical lines. A **plumb bob** helps you find plumb, while a **chalk line** allows you to quickly snap a straight line between two points. Mark walls for layouts with **color pencils** that match your paint or glaze colors, so you don't have to worry about erasing guidelines and measuring points.

Cotton cloths

Terry cloth

Plumb bob

Chalk line

Chamois cloth

Cheesecloth

Metal straightedge or ruler

Metal tape measure

Plastic bags

Kitchen sponge

Color pencils

Tight-pore cellulose sponge

Sea sponge

Paper bags

For many decorative paint projects, the rollers and brushes you use are critical for producing the texture, detail, and richness of the finish. Specialty rollers and brushes tend to be expensive, so buy only the tools you need for a specific project.

SHARE YOUR TOOLS

When you aren't likely to repeat a technique or a color scheme on another project, consider sharing your decorative painting tools and supplies with other do-it-yourselfers. Most decorative painting tools can be washed and reused for numerous projects. And by offering to share, you may be able to borrow some new-to-you supplies as well.

6-inch weaver brush

Wide wallpaper brush

Softening brush

Strié brush

Chip brush

Stippling brush

Artist's brush

Floppy roller

Extra-long-nap roller

Double roller tray

Double roller

Texturizing wire-loop roller

STENCILING TOOLS

tenciling requires several special tools and paint products. The most essential supplies include the following items.

Reusable, repositionable **stencils** are made of thin sheets of plastic, vinyl, or acetate. (Avoid paper stencils; paint will quickly destroy them.) Some stencils are precut, while others require you to cut out the images with a sharp **crafts knife** or **utility knife.**

Predesigned stencils feature motifs that can be applied as single images, repeating **borders,** or repeating **wallpaper-size patterns.** You can draw on **plain stencil acetate** with a permanent marker, then cut out your design with a knife or scissors. Adhere stencils to a wall or other surface with repositionable adhesive, typically available in a spray can. You also can use painter's tape to position stencils.

Thick-handled and tubular **stencil brushes** are available in a range of diameters and bristle types. The bristles should be tightly bundled together; bluntly, yet evenly, cut; and quite stiff. **Stencil paints** are available as gels, liquids, creams, and stick solids. Each type of paint produces a slightly different color and texture when applied to a surface.

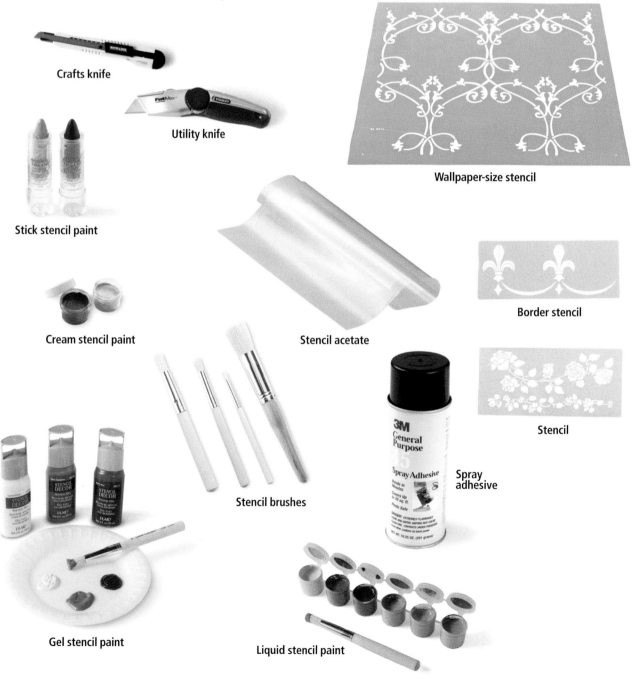

Crafts knife

Utility knife

Wallpaper-size stencil

Stick stencil paint

Border stencil

Cream stencil paint

Stencil acetate

Stencil

Stencil brushes

Spray adhesive

Gel stencil paint

Liquid stencil paint

SPECIALTY TOOLS

Specialty tools are those you use only for one or two specific decorative painting treatments.

Wood-graining tools, or rockers, typically have a curved head covered with a piece of ridged rubber. Dragging and rocking the tool through wet glaze produces wavy patterns that resemble wood grain. **Paint combs** are ridged rubber tools that you can drag through wet glaze to produce several effects. Combs are available as squeegee-style tools and as smaller handheld disks. The thickness and number of ridges vary.

Paint mitts are among the several tools that are covered with fabric strips or knots and produce a soft texture. Paint mitts are useful when applying finish to turned legs and other surfaces that are difficult to paint with a brush or roller.

Large **feathers** produce the undulating veins in faux marble treatments. **Foam stamps** can be loaded with paint and pressed onto surfaces to produce graphic images.

Decorative paint treatments that incorporate plaster, joint compound, or drywall compound require several special tools. A **trowel** mixes compound and produces rough texture when used to apply compound to a surface. A **4- to 6-inch drywall knife** spreads on compound in thin, smooth layers. A **putty knife** applies small amounts of compound to a surface or can be used to load a larger knife with compound. Venetian plaster is applied with thin, precision-ground **steel spatulas** in various sizes. A rectangular **plaster or drywall trough** holds two to four cups of mixed compound. Most troughs feature a steel edge that enables you to clean excess compound from your trowel or knife. (Because plaster and drywall compound dry out quickly, always mix a compound in a separate plastic mixing container and then load the trough with a small amount of prepared compound.)

BUY FOR A PROJECT

Buy specialty decorative painting supplies, such as the ones featured on these pages, with a specific project in mind. While these tools produce fantastic effects, they aren't worth the investment if the tool or paint is just going to sit in a drawer or closet unused.

Trough

Venetian plaster spatulas

Paint mitt

Feathers

Paint comb

Wood-graining tool

Putty knife

Foam stamps

Trowel

Drywall knife

PAINT, GLAZE, AND OTHER MATERIALS

For maximum durability and rich, true color, use high-quality paints, glazes, and other materials for your decorative painting projects. For easy application and cleanup, select **latex (water-base) paint** products. Latex paint is typically sold in quarts, gallons, and five-gallon containers. If you're trying a brand of paint for the first time, consider purchasing a sample portion (typically $5 or less). Apply the paint to sample boards (see page 41) and judge the paint's coverage, ease of application, and drying time.

Latex glazes are sold in quart and gallon metal cans and plastic jugs. The jugs are ideal for pouring glaze into mixing containers. Many paint brands also offer coordinating glazes, but you can mix latex paints and glazes from various manufacturers as you need. Manufacturers describe the look of their glazes in a host of ways—pearlescent, opalescent, metallic, and antique are some of the more common—all of which can be quite confusing. Purchase a small size of any new glaze and test it on a sample board before applying it to a project or actual surface.

Acrylic artist's paints (available in tubes and small containers at crafts and hobby stores) are perfect when you need a small amount of a color or when you want to slightly alter the tint of a larger quantity of paint or glaze. Powder pigments and universal tints are concentrated color that you mix with latex paint or glaze to produce custom colors. Add small quantities of **paint extender** to latex paint to increase the amount of time you can work with paint before it dries. Combine pouches of various solid additives—including **glitter, granite crystals,** and **tiny plastic beads**—with latex paint for custom textures and sheens. **Metallic leaf** is available as a concentrated liquid with suspended metal particles that you brush onto a surface, or as thin sheets of metal that you stick to a surface treated with **adhesive sizing.**

Polyurethane protects surfaces and seals them from moisture. Polyurethane is available in latex or oil-base formulas, tinted or clear. Several sheens are available also.

STORING PAINT

Paint, glaze, and other materials can be stored for a few months to about two years, if they are kept in a dry location and don't freeze or become overheated. Always refer to the manufacturer's label to determine how long and where to store paint products.

Glitter

Granite crystals

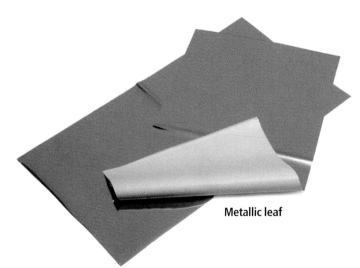
Metallic leaf

Paint extender

Opalescent glaze

Polyurethane varnish

Pearlescent glaze

Latex paint

Metallic glaze

Acrylic artist's paints

Painting
BASICS

Basic painting skills are the foundation of all the decorative painting techniques featured in this book. This section shows the essentials for repairing, preparing, priming, and painting almost every surface in a room. These tips will help you create an ideal canvas on which to apply almost any decorative painting technique. Painting a room has become easier, thanks to high-quality latex paints that are easy to apply and clean up. Improvements in brushes, rollers, and even mixing containers and trays make it possible for first-time painters to achieve professional-looking results.

The key to successfully painting a room—and, especially, painting a decorative finish—is planning. Before jumping into any paint project, even something as small as painting a flea-market end table, assess the situation. Evaluate the condition of the room or project you're about to undertake: Do you need to make any repairs or remove any existing finishes? Determine what paints and glazes you'll use and estimate how much of each you'll need to complete the project. Check that your tools and protective supplies, such as drop cloths and various types of tape, are all in good condition and sufficient quantities. Make a list of any supplies you need to purchase. (See Part 2 of this book for detailed information on shopping for paint.)

COLOR ON THE WALLS
Use both paint brushes and rollers to quickly cover walls with a smooth coat of colorful paint.

START WITH SPACKLE
Repair all nail holes, drywall screw pops, cracks, and other surface blemishes with spackling compound while preparing a room for decorative painting.

PATCH SMALL HOLES
Patch small to medium-size holes with scrap wood and drywall, cover with drywall compound, and finish to create a smooth surface for painting.

TAPE DOORS AND WINDOWS
Protect woodwork from paint splatters and clean up your paint project quickly by applying painter's tape around door and window frames.

DETAIL THE TRIM
Apply a smooth coat of semi-gloss paint to trim, molding, and window and door frames.

EXTEND YOUR REACH
Use an extension rod and long-nap roller to give a textured ceiling a bright coat of paint.

REPAIRING CRACKS, NAIL HOLES, AND POPPED FASTENERS

Walls in old and new homes undergo damage from changes in heat and moisture, foundation settling, and everyday use. Before investing the time and money to paint a room, repair cracks, holes, or popped nails or screws. Fortunately, most wall repairs—when done correctly—are simple, fast, and long-lasting.

The repair techniques featured here are shown on drywall surfaces. To repair drywall effectively, you need to remove paper backing material that's damaged and readily apparent. Bunched-up paper backing results in an uneven finished surface, even after spackling compound is spread on the drywall. Also, spackling compound bonds best with the gypsum that's underneath the paper backing, so removing the damaged paper makes a stronger repair. Plaster walls can be repaired easily as well. See the tip box on the opposite page.

FILL SMALL HOLES.

Remove bunched-up paper backing around the hole. Apply spackling compound inside and around the hole with a 3-inch drywall knife. Smooth and blend the transition from compound to drywall with the knife. Wet compound may bulge out a bit, but as it dries, it shrinks. Let dry, following manufacturer's instructions. Sand lightly. Spread on a second thin coat, if desired.

FILL CRACKS.

Remove any damaged paper or drywall around the crack with a paint scraper or utility knife. Using a 3-inch drywall knife, spread on a thin coat of spackling compound, following the direction of the crack. Let dry.

YOU'LL NEED

TIME: A few minutes to several hours, depending on the damage and the number of coats of spackling compound required.

SKILLS: No special skills.

TOOLS: Drywall knife, sanding block, sandpaper, 5-in-1 tool or flat-head screwdriver, utility knife, paint scraper, drill/driver (optional).

MATERIALS: Spackling compound.

SAND SMOOTH.

Sand dried compound with a sanding block and fine- or very fine-grit sandpaper. Press lightly so you don't scratch the surrounding surface. Spread on a second thin coat of compound, if desired. For medium- to large-size repairs, apply a stain-blocking primer to prepare the surface to receive paint.

TEXTURED WALLS

You have several options when applying decorative paint treatments to textured walls. You can prime textured surfaces and apply a treatment atop the texture. This saves time, but textured finishes can diminish the effect of many decorative paint treatments. Alternately, you can sand the texture down or off completely, then prime and paint. This option is time-consuming and produces a lot of dust. However, it may be your only option if the surface has extreme texture. Finally, you can float two or three thinned layers of drywall compound over the texture, filling in low spots and yielding a smooth finish.

DRIVE POPPED SCREWS AND NAILS.

For popped drywall screws, remove the damaged drywall and then use a screwdriver or drill/driver to drive the raised screw farther into the wall. Drive popped nailheads farther into the wall with a hammer and a nail set.

SPREAD ON SPACKLING COMPOUND.

Spread a thin coat of spackling compound in and around the hole with a 3-inch knife. Sand the repair smooth after the compound dries.

REPAIRS AND PREPARATIONS FOR SPECIAL SURFACES

Although the majority of modern walls are drywall, decorative painters may encounter other types of walls. Creating surfaces that are stable, clean, and as smooth as possible is worth the investment of your time. Here are some tips for other kinds of walls you may need to repair and prepare before you begin a decorative painting project:

Plaster. Damage to plaster walls tends to spread beyond the hole or crack that is readily apparent. The plaster surrounding the damaged area is often weakened or crumbling as well. To effectively patch and repair plaster walls, you need to slightly enlarge the site of the original damage and create a base of solid plaster, which you can then repair. Use a 5-in-1 tool, flathead screwdriver, or other tool to remove the weakened plaster that surrounds any damaged area. Also, because plaster is more porous than drywall, apply spackling or joint compound in multiple, thin coats and allow additional drying time.

Masonry and concrete. If your room has exposed masonry, block, or poured concrete walls, be sure to prime with a latex paint formulated for these surfaces. Latex paints are thicker than regular wall paints and should fill any minor chips or cracks. For larger flaws, use a chisel and hammer to dig out any loose material, dust the hole, and wipe with a damp sponge or rag. Patch the area with cement or mortar mixed per manufacturer's directions. Allow cement to cure for one to two weeks, depending on manufacturer's instructions.

Wood paneling. Secure any bowed paneling with wood screws drilled into studs, if possible. Countersink screws and apply drywall compound. You can prime and apply decorative treatments directly onto paneling. If you desire a smooth surface, do not attempt to fill in paneling grooves with drywall compound. Instead, cover the paneling with special liner paper (available at home centers and wallpaper stores) and then apply primer and decorative paint treatment.

PATCHING HOLES IN DRYWALL

A hole in drywall generally looks much worse than it actually is. You don't need to call in a professional carpenter to fix, patch, and smooth a hole that's approximately 3 to 8 inches in diameter. The repair technique outlined here takes a few hours, spread over two or more days, but the result is a seamless, flat surface.

YOU'LL NEED

TIME: Three to four hours, spread over two to three days.

SKILLS: Working with drywall compound.

TOOLS: Carpenter's square, pencil, keyhole saw, tape measure, utility knife, metal straightedge, drywall knife, drywall trough, mixing container, drill/driver, sanding block, sandpaper.

MATERIALS: Scrap of 1x4 or 1x6 pine board, drywall scrap, drywall screws, drywall compound.

▼ CAUTION

When sanding large patches of drywall compound, you create a lot of dust. Always wear safety goggles and a sanding mask or respirator when sanding drywall compound.

1 MARK OFF THE AREA TO BE PATCHED.

Use a metal square and pencil to lay out a square or rectangle slightly larger than the hole.

3 PREPARE A WOOD REINFORCEMENT.

Cut a strip of thin wood (a scrap piece of 1x2 or 1x4 pine works well). The strip should be several inches longer than the height of the hole. Slip the board into the hole and position it so the board extends equally above and below the hole.

2 CUT OUT DRYWALL.

Start a small hole in the drywall with a utility knife, if necessary. Use a keyhole saw (or drywall saw) to cut around the four sides of the marked rectangle. Remove drywall rectangle.

ENLARGE HOLE TO FIX IT

To repair a hole in a plaster wall, use a chisel and rubber mallet to remove a square or rectangular area all around the hole. Use a carpenter's square and a utility knife to cut a plug from a piece of thin drywall board; the center portion of the plug should be slightly smaller than the area hole, with 2 inches of drywall paper bordering the center. Spread compound around the hole and the center portion of the plug. Press the plug into the hole and smooth the drywall paper flat with the wall. Let dry. Spread on a thin coat of compound, let dry, and sand. Prime the area with stain-blocking primer.

4 ATTACH THE WOOD.

Use a drill/driver to drive several drywall screws through the surrounding drywall into the reinforcement board.

5 CREATE A DRYWALL PATCH FOR THE HOLE.

Use a tape measure, utility knife, and metal straightedge to cut a piece of drywall to fit inside the hole.

6 SECURE THE PATCH.

Drive several screws through the drywall patch into the reinforcement board. Draw the patch down flush with the surrounding wall.

7 SPREAD ON COMPOUND.

Using a 3-inch drywall knife, spread a thin coat of drywall compound over the joint between the wall and patch. If necessary, apply drywall tape around the plug perimeter and spread on another thin coat of compound. Let dry. Sand with fine sandpaper.

8 APPLY SECOND COAT.

Use a 6-inch drywall knife to spread a second coat of drywall compound on the area, blending in the patched area with the surrounding wall. Let dry and sand.

9 APPLY THIRD COAT.

If desired (or if patching a hole more than 6 inches or so in diameter), use a 12-inch drywall knife to spread on a third coat of drywall compound. Let dry, sand lightly, prime, and paint.

CLEANING AND ROOM PREPARATION

Many latex paints have exceptional hiding ability, which means one or two coats of fresh paint can completely cover the original finish. Even high-hiding paints, however, don't cover pencil, ink, or stains caused by moisture or mildew. A thorough cleaning is required to prepare these surfaces for painting. Similarly, heavily damaged woodwork and surfaces that exhibit scaled or flaking paint need more than a light sanding and a fresh coat of paint. Fix the damage first; then prime and paint.

In addition to cleaning, preparing for painting includes protecting the floors, trim, and furniture in the room. You can use plastic, paper, and canvas sheeting to protect surfaces; each type of covering has its pros and cons. Applying painter's tape to moldings, trim, baseboards, and door and window frames is time-consuming, but the effort protects those surfaces from paint spatters and creates a crisp, clean line between trim and wall.

1 WASH AND WIPE DOWN SURFACES.

Use a cellulose sponge to wipe down stains with a solution of one part bleach to three parts water. Wear rubber gloves when working with bleach and consider wearing goggles if you're sensitive to bleach. Don't mix bleach with any other household cleaners. Unstained surfaces can be washed with a mild solution of TSP and water; rinse off the TSP with clean water. Let dry.

2 MAKE SMALL REPAIRS.

Fill any holes or gouges with wood putty. Let dry. If you plan to repaint painted woodwork, remove the surface gloss with a sanding block and fine-grit sandpaper. Wipe down sanded trim with wet rag or tack cloth to remove dust.

YOU'LL NEED

TIME: Half a day to prepare a 12×12 room.

SKILLS: No special skills.

TOOLS: Cellulose sponge, rags, bucket, rubber gloves, sanding block, sandpaper, painter's tape, drop cloths, plastic sheeting, short-nap roller cover, roller frame, roller tray.

MATERIALS: Soapy water, wood putty, trisodium phosphate, primer.

3 TAPE OFF BASE-BOARDS.

Apply 3-inch-wide painter's tape that is sticky along only one edge at the junction of the baseboard and the flooring. If you can, remove the baseboards instead, then sand and finish them. Reinstall them after the walls are painted.

PHOSPHATES

TSP, trisodium phosphate, is a nonsudsing soap available as a liquid solution or dry powder at home centers and hardware stores. Because TSP contains phosphates, which causes algae bloom in standing water, the chemical is restricted in some areas and should be used only when necessary. Follow the manufacturer's recommendations when mixing TSP with water, but typically $\frac{1}{4}$ cup in a gallon of water is good for general cleaning. Always rinse surfaces with clean water after washing them with TSP.

4 PROTECT FLOORS AND FURNITURE.

Lay out paper, plastic, or canvas drop cloths on the floor, covering the entire floor. Tuck edges of the cloth under the baseboard tape. Tape down sheeting to baseboard every 6 to 8 feet to ensure cloths stay in place. Wrap furniture in thin plastic sheeting; tape sheeting in place.

5 TAPE OFF DOOR AND WINDOW FRAMES.

If you plan to paint the walls first, apply 1-inch painter's tape around all door and window frames. Burnish the tape with your fingernail or a small plastic tool.

TINTED PRIMER

A dark paint color requires a tinted primer to prepare the surface and boost the bonding of the paint to the surface. Dark paint usually has lower hiding power than white paint, so it may take several coats to cover white primer. Primer that is a tint of the top-coat color is less likely to show through.

6 CUT IN THE PRIMER.

Brush on primer with a 4- to 6-inch paintbrush, starting at a corner and working around the room at the floor and ceiling lines. Work with a home center or paint store professional to determine the type of primer that's most appropriate for your project.

7 PRIME WALLS.

Roll on primer to larger areas of the room with a short-nap roller mounted on an extension rod. Let dry.

PRIMER VS. PAINT

Primer performs a different job than paint. Primer blocks out color and stains while providing a uniform base for paint to bond with the surface. Primer dries more quickly than regular paint and can include special ingredients to seal the surface, contain stains, or stop mold growth. Regular paint provides color and a durable, scrubbable surface.

PAINTING CEILINGS

A freshly painted ceiling completes a room makeover and ties the entire transformation together.

Whether you paint a ceiling bright white, off-white, or some other color, the technique for painting is the same. Most painters paint ceilings first so that any paint splatter that gets on the walls can be easily cleaned up or simply painted over when the walls receive their coat of paint.

YOU'LL NEED

TIME: Half a day to roll on one coat of paint to 150 square feet of ceiling.

SKILLS: Rolling on paint, overhead strength.

TOOLS: Long-nap roller cover, roller frame, trim brush, roller tray, extension rod, stepladder, painter's cap, safety glasses, painter's tape, drop cloths, plastic sheeting, rags.

MATERIALS: High-hiding latex ceiling paint.

① MASK OFF THE CEILING LINE.

If the walls are already painted or the room has crown molding, mask around the ceiling line with a band of 2- or 3-inch-wide painter's tape. Go all around the room.

② CUT IN THE EDGE.

Load a 3- to 5-inch paintbrush with paint and cut in the paint along the ceiling edge, starting at a corner. Brush on a generous band of paint about 6 inches wide on the ceiling. Continue brushing on paint around the perimeter of the room.

COLOR THE CEILING?

If you're concerned that a bright white ceiling will contrast too much with richly colored walls, consider painting the ceiling the lightest shade on the same paint strip from which you select the main wall color. The lightest shade will read to the eye as white (or nearly white) while blending perfectly with the rich color you paint on the walls. If you're feeling a bit more adventurous, consider painting the ceiling one shade lighter than the wall color. To bring the ceiling visually down and make a space feel more intimate, paint the ceiling one or two shades darker than the wall color.

CAUTION

To avoid getting paint in your eyes, always wear safety glasses or goggles while painting ceilings. Also, cover your hair with a bandanna or a brimmed painter's cap.

CAUTION

Shut off overhead fixtures at the breaker or fuse box before applying paint to a ceiling. Paint is a liquid and can conduct electricity. Remove overhead light fixtures, if possible, or wrap them in plastic bags and seal with painter's tape.

3 ROLL ON THE PAINT.

Fill a paint tray with ceiling paint. Mount a long-nap roller on an extension rod, load with ceiling paint, and roll paint, staying parallel to the wet, brushed-on edge. Reload the roller as needed.

4 ROLL IT AGAIN FOR EVEN COVERAGE.

Switch directions and roll on more paint perpendicular to the first roller pass. Doing so ensures more consistent coverage and often eliminates the need for a second coat of paint.

PAINTING POPCORN CEILINGS

If your home's ceilings have sprayed-on "popcorn" texture, you have some options when it comes time to repaint this surface. Whatever option you choose, it's important to remember that sprayed-on ceilings can contain asbestos. If you are unsure of whether your ceiling contains asbestos, purchase a test kit from a home center or have a professional test the surface. Asbestos can be safely painted, covered, or removed, but proper procedures must be followed. Visit www.epa.gov for more information.

The three main options for working with any textured ceiling are as follows:

Paint over the popcorn. Long-nap rollers are best for working paint into the rough, porous texture. Avoid shorter-nap rollers and foam rollers; they take twice the effort to cover the ceiling and cause more bits of

sprayed-on texture to fall off than long-nap rollers. Another option for painting over the texture is to rent a paint sprayer from a home center.

Cover the popcorn. Cover the ceiling with sheets of ⅛- to ½-inch drywall. Consult with a home center professional to determine the appropriate fasteners and cutting tools to use for the job. Attach drywall panels to joints or studs.

Remove the popcorn. Sprayed-on texture can be removed, but it is a messy job. Mix a solution of 1 cup liquid fabric softener, 1 cup ammonia, and 1 gallon water. Spray the solution onto the surface and let soak for 15 to 20 minutes. Scrap off the texture with a 12-inch drywall knife or wide window-washing squeegee. Be sure floors, trim, and furnishings are thoroughly covered with plastic drop cloths and sheets.

PAINTING WALLS

Much of the time working on a paint project involves using the basic wall-painting technique described here. To help the actual wall painting go as smoothly and quickly as possible, be sure to completely clean, repair, prepare, and prime the room to be painted before beginning to brush or roll on a top coat of paint. (See pages 144–149.)

YOU'LL NEED

TIME: Half a day to apply one coat of paint to a 12×12 room.

SKILLS: Rolling and brushing on paint, maintaining a wet edge.

TOOLS: Trim paintbrush, short-nap roller cover, roller frame, roller tray, extension rod, rags, stepladder, circulating fan (optional).

MATERIALS: Latex paint.

1 CUT IN THE CORNERS.

Beginning at a corner, cut in paint with a 2- or 3-inch trim brush. Use long strokes, smoothly blending each stroke into the next. Cut in only as much area as you will be able to roll on while still maintaining a wet edge.

2 CUT IN DOORS AND WINDOWS.

Brush on paint around taped-off door and window frames, continuing to use the same long stroke. For information about painting trim, see page 154.

GOT PAINT?

Before you start rolling on wall paint, double-check your quantity estimates and make sure you have enough paint to complete the number of coats that are necessary. If you do run out of paint, find a good stopping point. Stopping after applying a full coat to the entire room is best, but you also can finish an entire wall and stop at the corner. Avoid stopping at midwall.

3 CUT IN THE CEILING LINE.

Brush on paint at the line where the wall and ceiling meet. You can tape off the ceiling or you can carefully brush on paint at the ceiling line, if you have a steady hand. For information on painting ceilings, see page 150.

4 LOAD THE PAINT ROLLER.

Fill a paint tray with wall paint and load the roller, mounted on an extension rod, if desired. Roll on the first vertical strip of paint, working the roller into the wet brushed-on portion of the wall. Continue to roll on paint along the wet edges of the wall.

5 ROLL ON THE PAINT.

In the open, central area of the wall, roll on paint in a "W" or "M" pattern. Roll back over areas where you've applied paint to ensure complete coverage. Work in approximately 3-foot-square sections; then move down or across and roll on more paint, using the same motion.

6 MOVE TO THE NEXT SECTION.

When a section of wall is painted and still slightly wet, step back 8 to 10 feet and evaluate the coverage. Roll back over areas where the paint seems thin. Let dry. Allow paint to cure, ideally for 24 hours. Brush another coat of paint around edges and then roll on the second coat.

PAINTING TRIM

Almost everything about painting trim takes patience and time. Most trim needs to be prepared (repaired, sanded, and possibly primed) before it can receive a top coat of paint. (Refer to page 148 for more information.) Brushing paint onto narrow surfaces, intricate details, or moving elements, such as window sashes and door hinges, takes a steady hand.

YOU'LL NEED

TIME: Half a day.

SKILLS: Preparing wood to receive paint, masking off, brushing on paint.

TOOLS: Sandpaper, sanding block, wire brush (optional), rags, painter's tape, angled trim brush.

MATERIALS: Wood putty or filler, primer appropriate for bare wood.

1 DEGLOSS THE TRIM.

Sand the surface sheen off painted trim. Sand flat areas with a sanding block and fine-grit sandpaper. To sand rounded or detailed portions of trim, wrap a piece of sandpaper around your fingers or fold it into a pad and work the sandpaper as deep into the trim as possible.

2 REMOVE LOOSE CHIPS AND PAINT.

Use a wire brush or medium-grit sandpaper to remove loose, chipped, or cracked paint. If the old paint around a window or door frame is loose, figure out the cause of the problem. Remedy any moisture- or heat-related problems before repainting the window or door.

KEEP A RAG AROUND

Carry a clean, damp rag in your back pocket or free hand. The moment you brush beyond the area that should receive paint, wipe the erroneous application off with the rag; then try again.

3 REPAIR TRIM.

Fill any cracks or holes in the trim with wood putty. Wood putty is available in a stick or a paste form. Follow manufacturer's instructions and let dry.

4 SEAL CRACKS AND GAPS.

If there are gaps in the mitered corners of window and door casings, fill them with paintable water-base caulk. Wipe off excess caulk with a wet rag. Let dry.

5 SAND AND WIPE-DOWN.

Sand any areas where putty or filler has been applied. Wipe the surface with a clean, damp cloth or tack cloth.

6 TAPE THE TRIM.

Apply 1-inch painter's tape to the wall around the trim to be painted. Burnish the tape with your fingernail or a plastic tool to ensure a tight fit.

7 BRUSH ON THE PAINT.

Brush on the first coat of paint with an angled trim brush. Use long strokes and follow the grain of the wood. Let dry. If you're painting operable trim, such as windows or doors, check that these features have not been painted shut after paint dries for an hour or so. Apply a second coat of paint, if desired.

GLOSSARY

For words not listed here or for more about those that are, refer to the index, pages 158–160.

Accent color. A hue in a color scheme that, although used in moderation, grabs attention.

Acrylic. A synthetic substance in paint that acts as a binder and makes the paint durable and fade-resistant.

Additive. Ingredient in paint that gives the paint additional capabilities, such as scrubability or sun-resistance.

Additive technique. Any decorative paint technique in which paint or glaze is applied to a surface.

Alkyd paint. Oil-base paint.

Artist's color. Acrylic or oil paint used by artists, usually thick paste in a tube. Some acrylic artist's paints are available as liquids in small bottles.

Asbestos. Common building material used in fiberboards, insulation, and other products prior to 1970. Asbestos must be handled or removed carefully with assistance from an asbestos abatement contractor.

Binder. Paint ingredient that holds additives and pigments to the surface.

Chair-rail height. The area 32 to 36 inches from the floor on a wall that is a visually appealing location for decorative molding or paint treatments.

Chamois. Soft leather made from sheepskin; also a thick, soft cotton fabric that imitates chamois leather. Chamois cloth often is used in decorative painting.

Cheesecloth. Lightweight, loosely woven cotton cloth.

Chip brush. An inexpensive brush that looks like a paintbrush, but is made primarily for sweeping rather than painting.

Coverage. The surface area that a given amount of paint can cover.

Double roller. A paint roller that applies two colors at one time.

Eggshell. A low-luster paint sheen.

Extender. A paint additive that increases working time.

Faux. Imitation or fake, from the French word for "false." Pronounced "foe."

Ferrule. Metal band on a paintbrush that bundles bristles around the handle.

Flagging. The split ends on the bristles of a paintbrush. A brush with more flagging can hold more paint.

Flat. Nonreflective paint sheen with a muted appearance.

Flyspecks. Tiny, dark flecks produced by insects and age. Simulated in decorative painting with paint spatters.

Fresco. A traditional technique in which paint is applied to a wet layer of plaster.

Frottage. A technique in which a sheet of paper or plastic is pressed into wet paint and then removed.

Glaze. Thin, semitransparent latex paint, applied as a top coat.

Gloss. Shiny, reflective paint sheen.

Hardboard. Thin, dense wood-composite material, often used as paneling.

Kraft paper. Brown, heavier-weight paper, sold in rolls. Can be used as a floor cloth. Also known as craft paper.

Latex. Water-base paint.

Lead. A toxic ingredient found in most paints prior to 1950. Lead limits were set for paint in 1978. Any paint older than 1978 should be tested for lead content.

Level. A line that is perfectly parallel with the horizon, usually found by using a tool, also called a level.

Masking off. Applying tape, paper, or plastic to a surface that you don't want paint applied to.

Matte. Another word to describe a flat sheen.

Moiré. A pattern of wavy lines, running in one direction.

Nap. The thickness and length of the fibers on a paint roller.

Nylon abrasive pad. A fine, woven abrasive in a dense pad that substitutes for steel wool. Preferable to steel wool when working with water-base paints and glazes because particles that become embedded in the surface won't make rust spots.

Painter's tape. Lower-tack masking tape preferred by painters because it applies more easily and doesn't remove paint or other finishes when lifted. The tape is usually blue.

Pigment. Solid paint ingredient that gives the paint its color.

Plumb. A true vertical line, usually found with a plumb bob or a string with one weighted end.

Pom-pom. A piece of fabric held in a tight cluster, used to apply glaze to a surface.

Pounce. Applying paint by pressing a rag, sponge, or other applicator onto the surface.

Primer. A coat of paint that prepares the surface for the application of a top coat of paint.

Sample board. A 1- to 2-foot-square of hardboard or plywood, primed and painted to resemble a wall surface. Sample boards give you an opportunity to refine your technique, as well as test color and product combinations.

Satin. A low-luster paint sheen, usually more reflective than eggshell.

Semigloss. Slightly shiny and reflective paint sheen.

Sheen. The reflectivity of a coat of paint.

Smoke-stained. A coat of medium- to dark-brown glaze applied to a surface that mimics the look of extreme age and wear.

Stencil. Plastic or heavy paper sheet material with a design cut into it. Paint forced through the cutout design makes an impression on a surface.

Stipple. To texture paint with numerous small, quick, straight strokes of a brush or stippling tool.

Strié. Dragging a dry brush through a wet glaze top coat, revealing streaks of paint below.

Subtractive technique. Any decorative painting technique where paint or glaze is applied to a surface and then removed.

Suede. Soft leather with a napped surface. A decorative paint finish that imitates the look of suede.

Sun-faded. A coat of light gold or brown glaze applied to a surface to mimic the look of extended sunlight exposure.

Tea-stained. A coat of light- to medium-brown glaze applied to a surface to mimic the look of fabric dipped in strong tea.

TSP. Trisodium phosphate, a chemical used as a cleaning agent.

Venetian plaster. A decorative technique that employs several thin layers of tinted plaster.

Verdigris. Green and turquoise coloration that copper metal takes on when exposed to water and sun. Also a painting technique that imitates this look.

Wainscot. A wall surface divided horizontally, with the top and bottom portions having different wall treatments. Also referred to as wainscoting.

Wet edge. Undried portion of an area of paint.

Workability. How long paint remains wet enough for you to complete the paint technique.

INDEX

Index (continued)

METRIC CONVERSIONS

U.S. Units to Metric Equivalents			Metric Units to U.S. Equivalents		
To convert from	Multiply by	To Get	To convert from	Multiply by	To Get
Inches	25.4	Millimeters	Millimeters	0.0394	Inches
Inches	2.54	Centimeters	Centimeters	0.3937	Inches
Feet	30.48	Centimeters	Centimeters	0.0328	Feet
Feet	.03048	Meters	Meters	3.2808	Feet
Yards	.9144	Meters	Meters	1.0936	Yards
Miles	1.6093	Kilometers	Kilometers	0.6214	Miles
Square inches	6.4516	Square centimeters	Square centimeters	0.1550	Square inches
Square feet	0.0929	Square meters	Square meters	10.764	Square feet
Square yards	0.8361	Square meters	Square meters	1.1960	Square yards
Acres	0.4047	Hectares	Hectares	2.4711	Acres
Square miles	2.5899	Square kilometers	Square kilometers	0.3861	Square miles
Cubic inches	16.387	Cubic centimeters	Cubic centimeters	0.0610	Cubic inches
Cubic feet	0.0283	Cubic meters	Cubic meters	35.315	Cubic feet
Cubic feet	28.316	Liters	Liters	0.0353	Cubic feet
Cubic yards	0.7646	Cubic meters	Cubic meters	1.038U	Cubic yards
Cubic yards	764.55	Liters	Liters	0.0013	Cubic yards

To convert from degrees Fahrenheit (F) to degrees Celsius (C), first subtract 32, then multiply by ⅚.

To convert from degrees Celsius to degrees Fahrenheit, multiply by ⅚, then add 32.